STOKED

FIRING UP
YOUR PASSION
FOR GOD

DANNY LEHMANN
WITH SCOTT TOMPKINS

PUBLISHING
A Ministry Of Youth With A Mission

P.O. Box 55787, S

D1054062

YWAM Publishing is the publishing ministry of Youth With A Mission. Youth With A Mission (YWAM) is an international missionary organization of Christians from many denominations dedicated to presenting Jesus Christ to this generation. To this end, YWAM has focused its efforts in three main areas:
1) Training and equipping believers for their part in fulfilling the Great Commission (Matthew 28:19). 2) Personal evangelism. 3) Mercy ministry (medical and relief work).
For a free catalog of books and materials write or call:
YWAM Publishing
P.O. Box 55787, Seattle, WA 98155
(206)771-1153 or (800) 922-2143
e-mail address: 75701.2772 @ compuserve.com

Verses marked AMP are taken from The Amplified Bible, Old Testament, Copyright © 1965 and 1987 by The Zondervan Corporation, and from The Amplified New Testament, Copyright © 1954, 1958, 1987 by the Lockman Foundation. Used by permission.
Verses marked KJV are taken from the King James Version of the Bible.
Verses marked NAS are taken from the New American Standard Bible, © 1960, 1962, 1963, 1968, 1971, 1972, 1973, 1975, 1977 by the Lockman Foundation. Used by permission.
Verses marked NEB are taken from The New English Bible, © The Delegates of the Oxford University Press and the Syndics of the Cambridge University Press 1961, 1970. Reprinted with permission.
Verses marked NIV are taken from the Holy Bible, New International Version®, Copyright © 1973, 1978, 1984 by the International Bible Society. Used by permission of Zondervan Publishing House. The "NIV" and "New International Version" trademarks are registered in the United States Patent and Trademark Office by International Bible Society.
Verses marked NKJV are taken from the New King James Version, Copyright © 1979, 1980, 1982 by Thomas Nelson, Inc., Publishers. Used by permission.
Verses marked PHILLIPS are taken from J.B. Phillips: The New Testament in Modern English, Revised Edition. © J.B. Phillips 1958, 1960, 1972. Used by permission of Macmillan Publishing Company.
Verses marked RSV are taken from the Revised Standard Version of the Bible, Copyright 1946, 1952, 1971 by the Division of Christian Education of the National Council of the Churches of Christ in the U.S.A. Used by permission.

STOKED — Firing Up Your Passion For God
Copyright ©1997 Danny Lehmann

Published by Youth With A Mission Publishing
P.O. Box 55787
Seattle, WA 98155

ISBN 0-927545-93-4

Printed in the United States of America.

Dedication

In the summer of 1970 I was a confused teenager sitting alone on a fence outside Mueller's Bar on Washington Blvd. in Balitmore, Maryland. Out of nowhere my father, Carl Lehmann, appeared from around the corner. Our eyes met. Both of us in our own way were trying to deal with the recent loss of my mom to cancer. Spontaneously he asked me, "What are you doing, son?" To which I confidently responded, "Waitin' for somethin' to happen!" Then with a lot of fatherly love and a little prophetic punch he said, "Why don't you go out and make something happen?"

Those words have stuck with me ever since then, especially at times when I'm just "sitting on a fence" in one form or another "Waitin' for somethin' to happen." In many ways, over the years my dad has been an inspiration to me to have a healthy disdain for fence-sitting and a desire to be "stoked" about whatever I put my hand to. (Like the time he ran the Honolulu Marathon at age 73 on a broken toe!)

It's to him and all those readers who tend to be fence-sitters who need to hear his advice that I joyfully dedicate this book. "Why don't you go out and make something happen?!"

Contents

Foreword

In *Stoked*, Danny Lehmann shares with us not only how to get the fire of God into our hearts, but how to keep it burning brightly and passionately.

My firm conviction is that things will get darker in the days ahead. If we are going to survive and indeed flourish as Christians, our flame is going to have to burn brighter. That is why I welcome this new book by Danny. I am confident it will challenge, encourage, and motivate us to a deeper commitment to Christ, resulting in a greater passion to serve Him.

Danny is not sitting in some ivory tower lecturing down to us. Having known him for a number of years, I can honestly say he is a man who practices what he preaches. *He is* a man who is truly "stoked."

Greg Laurie
President of Harvest Crusades

Acknowledgments

As the author of a book about zeal, I must humbly acknowledge those who have stoked my fire for God and encouraged me during the long months of researching, writing and editing. My only fear in mentioning names is that I may leave someone out, but at that risk, I want to honor those to whom honor is due.

Although this book is dedicated to my natural father, I would like to honor and thank my two "spiritual fathers," Chuck Smith and Loren Cunningham. Through the years, they have fired my passion for God through both their example and instruction. I am only one of thousands touched by these men of God. Through their two contemporary movements—Calvary Chapel and Youth With A Mission—they have ignited spiritual fires that are blazing all over the planet. May their tribes multiply!

I would also like to acknowledge some who are no longer with us, but whose writings and legacy are still causing Christians to catch fire. Those who have most inspired me include William and Catherine Booth, Charles Finney, John Wesley, Charles Spurgeon and Dwight Moody.

Then there are more contemporary saints, who through their passing on to glory, have also awakened me to the need to keep my fire burning. They include Keith Green, Lonnie Frisbee, Bryce Enns, Romila Rana and Alan Williams. In their own ways, each poured holy fuel on my burning heart.

Contemporary writers Gordon MacDonald, Michael Green, John Stott, Floyd McClung and George Verwer have also contributed to this volume through their spiritual insights. Mario Murillo's message on "Generation X and the Thirty-Year Curse" got me started on the material that became Chapter 11. Winkey Pratney's research and teaching on revival helped catalyze my thinking on the subject. Meanwhile, Steve Gregg's teaching opened up my understanding of the "Parable of the Unprofitable Servant" (see Chapter 7).

Finally, many thanks to Scott Tompkins, who bailed me out when I was in desperate need of an editor, and who wielded his editing scissors with compassion! I also want to thank Kim Hall, my faithful, phlegmatic secretary, who worked tirelessly on this project, and Greg Laurie for writing the foreword.

Sola Gloria Dei,

Danny Lehmann
Honolulu, Hawaii

Introduction

Catching God's New Wave

Cold Pacific water dripped from my long, sun-bleached hair as I planted my surfboard in the sand, and stopped to soak in the first few rays of misty morning sun. I'd just surfed "The Hook," one of the top rides on the wave-rich east side of Santa Cruz, and just thinking about it gave me a rush.

I had left Baltimore at 18, and set out for this promised land of California sun, sand and surf. Days like today confirmed my choice in a dozen ways. "The Hook" was surfers' Nirvana. Its churning blue-green waters seductively invited us to come and play, and once you caught one of its thundering, crescent-shaped waves, you *were* hooked on the place. The waves exploded off huge north swells, driven down by storms born in the Gulf of Alaska. In back of the beach were majestic eucalyptus trees that towered over cliffs with cascades of shiny ice plant. The sun now burst through the fog like a crowning jewel over Monterey Bay.

I revelled in the scene, watching my friends carve the glassy, tubular mountains of water and anticipating my next surf session. Like many surfers on "Pleasure Point" (the neighborhood surrounding "The Hook"), I was a self-satisfied, carefree guy whose lifestyle revolved around the fickle moves of Mother Ocean. I felt strangely grateful for this easy life, but gave no thought to whom I should be thankful. Against this backdrop came a five-minute encounter that radically altered my life.

While I was getting ready to pull on my O'Neills' wet suit and hit the waves again, two local surfers approached unexpectedly. Kevin and Kelly, identical twins, offered a broad smile and a free newspaper. The paper was similar to many "underground" papers

I'd seen. These papers championed causes ranging from over-throwing the U.S. government, to the how-to's of Kundulini Yoga, and the legalization of marijuana.

This paper's headline and graphics instantly caught my eye. On the front page was a hip-looking cartoon about the second coming of Christ with surfers flying off their boards into the sky. In big, bold letters it said: "STOKED ON JESUS." The headline stopped me in my tracks. Noticing my surprise, Kevin asked if I was a Christian. "Sure, isn't everybody?" I replied. Before he had a chance to answer, I said, "What is a Christian anyway?" They responded with a joy that seemed contagious: "A Christian is somebody who's stoked on Jesus!"

As a surfer, I often used the word stoked. To me and thousands of others, it meant excited, enthusiastic, committed to the point of absolute abandonment to the object of the "stoke," which in our case were waves that cried out to be ridden. To be stoked meant that a job, a girlfriend, a family commitment or even final exams would have to take a back seat if the waves were up. Nothing short of a nuclear bomb could quench the adrenaline-pumping, heart-pounding, single-minded fervor of a surfer who is stoked.

The definition of the word in my beach culture left me scratching my salty head as I walked home with my surfboard in one hand and the *Hollywood Free Paper* in the other. STOKED—I understood that. It related to life, fun, and a natural and emotional "high" that comes from deep within and fires you like a boiler on a ship or wood to a furnace. But—STOKED ON JESUS? How does He fit in? To me Jesus was cool, a kind of First Century flower child who spoke of love and peace. He had a lot of good things to say, but so did Mohammed, Confucius and Buddha.

The image of Jesus I knew most was the anguished figure on the crucifix above the altar at St. Jerome's Catholic Church in Baltimore. It seemed like the proper thing to keep Jesus behind the altar rail, where He could be venerated on Sunday mornings and selected holidays. Growing up in the church, I came to view religion as a lot of formalism and tradition. Even so, it seemed a good thing—as long as you didn't become too fanatical about it. That's why the words "stoked" and "Jesus" struck me as so strange. It was an oxymoron—two words that just don't go together.

Some hours later, while sprawled out on the floor of my rented A-frame house on Pleasure Point's 36th Avenue, I devoured the contents of the *Hollywood Free Paper*. In one article, Margo Godfrey, then the reigning woman's World Surfing Champion, testified that having made it to the top of the surfing world hadn't fulfilled her deepest need. She found that only Jesus could satisfy. Another top surfer entitled his article, "I loved surfing with all my heart, and it never loved me back." There were testimonies and stories that seemed like "interest doors" into my own heart and life. The articles were as diverse as they could be, but they all pointed in one direction—UP!

Reading the odd-looking Gospel paper started me on a six-month spiritual journey in which I searched for God in the Bible, nature, the church, rock music and contemporary gurus, which were abundant in Santa Cruz. I also explored a cult, listened to a televised Billy Graham crusade and watched a re-run of Cecil B. DeMille's epic movie, "The Ten Commandments."

My conclusion was this: If Jesus Christ is who He says He is, and did what He said He did, then it was only reasonable that I be infinitely more "stoked" on Him than I should be on surfing or anything else. On a warm, moonlit summer night, I got on my knees in the sand about 100 yards down the beach from where I first heard about being stoked on Jesus. I don't remember the words of my prayer, but a few lines from Randy Stonehill's song, "First Prayer," express what was in my heart:

> *Lord, I really don't know how to pray*
> *But you know what I'm trying to say*
> *I don't want my life to end*
> *Not really knowing why it began.*

That night, my life took a radical turn.

Twenty years have flown by since that encounter on the beach. Many "zeal stealers" and "stoke chokers" have crossed my path and tried—and sometimes succeeded—in quenching my love for God and my fellow man. I've been persecuted, ridiculed, threatened, and humiliated by non-Christians. I have been betrayed, ripped off, slandered and lied to by professing Christians. I have been let down by Christian leaders who proved to be hypocrites, and fed false doctrine by some Bible teachers who tried to draw away disciples after themselves, rather than the Lord. At times in my Christian life, I have swung between extremes of legalism and loose living, arrogant pride and wimpy false humility, agnosticism and apathy. And often, these extremes have thrown cold water on holy fire.

But, today, by God's grace, I'm still stoked on Jesus. I am more excited about following Christ now than when I first received Him. There is but one reason—HE NEVER CHANGES! He has been faithful to save my soul and heal my mind from the ravages of LSD, taken in my teen years in an attempt to expand my consciousness. He has also provided me with a wonderful family and ministry, and supplied all the needs of both.

As I have reached out to others, I've seen Him change lives, heal minds and bodies, set captives free, provide for and release missionaries, and work His wonders in a thousand other ways. When I have blown it, He has "covered" for me. When I have been faithless, He has remained faithful, and He's proved His promises true countless times. Just as it says in Philippians 1:6 (NIV), "he who began a good work in you will carry it on to completion until the day of Christ Jesus."

How about you? Are you stoked? Are you excited about loving Jesus and serving Him? Can you, like Jehu, reach down and take the hand of a younger Christian, pull him up on your chariot and invite him to "Come with me, and see my zeal for the Lord" (2 Kings 10:16 KJV)? Can you, like Paul, boldly challenge others to follow you as you follow Christ (1 Cor. 11:1)? If not, why not?

The late U.S. Sen. Robert Kennedy once said, "Some people see things as they are and ask 'Why?' I look at things the way they could be and say 'Why Not?'" We need to ask that question of ourselves sometimes and start seeing things through eyes of faith.

Could God work in us such a change that we would voluntarily abandon our personal comforts and pour out our lives for the lost and needy? Why not? Could God actually turn us from self-centered, navel-gazing, worry-warts into fearless Christian warriors?

Why not? Can the power of God once again raise up the church as the light of the world and send out apostolic flame-throwers of His love to every nation on earth? Why not?

The Holy Spirit wants to send the same fire that came down from heaven on the day of Pentecost into your heart, so it can burn its way down into your soul. He wants to set you on fire so you, in turn, can help spread the flame around the world. On that glorious day when the Lord returns, may He find us all STOKED ON JESUS.

A Zealot's Prayer

"God give me a deep humility, a well-guided zeal, a burning love and a single eye, and then let men and devils do their worst!"

George Whitefield

Chapter One

Igniting the Flame

"...Our God is a consuming fire"
Heb. 12:29 (KJV)

Ever since the first caveman rubbed two sticks together and discovered fire, mankind has commonly seen both the usefulness and destructive power of fire.

Depending on the situation, fire can be the source of deepest comfort or greatest dread. In the burn unit of any major hospital, you'll find people suffering some of the most intense pain known to humanity because of fire. On the other hand, a fire's warmth can be a lifesaver for someone lost in an icy wilderness. Our perspective largely depends on how we've encountered fire and its effects.

The Bible portrays fire in the same good/bad, love/hate, can't live with it/or without it paradox. The most horrible description of human suffering is the hideous eternal lake of fire described in Revelation. Fire in the Bible often symbolizes the judgment and wrath of an Almighty God. While God promised Noah He'd never

17

again judge the Earth with a flood, the threat of fiery judgment looms like a guillotine over a world gone mad with sin. Only God's incredible patience spares the world from the cleansing fire its sin deserves. The Bible says Jesus will return in "flaming fire" (2 Thes. 1:7) and the Earth will be incinerated (2 Peter 3:10).

Yet Jesus also uses fire as an illustration of the glowing passion He would ignite in the hearts of His followers. In Luke 12:49 (NIV) He says: "I have come to bring fire on the earth, and how I wish it were already kindled." Jesus knew full well the strong imagery of this metaphor. In context it speaks of how the Holy Spirit's fire will set ablaze His disciples and cause a fiery division between those who follow Christ and those who oppose Him.

This and many other Scripture passages clearly show that it is God's will for us to have a burning spiritual passion. The issue for most of us is in deciding to fully yield ourselves to God so He can fill us with that passion.

Jesus illustrates it as a choice of two roads—a narrow road that those with a blazing love for God follow to heaven, and a broad one on which we follow our burning lusts into hell. However, we 20th century Christians seem to have invented a third road. It's not too narrow—that's for missionaries, monks and martyrs—and it's not too broad—that's for pimps, prostitutes and perverts. It's right in between.

Those who would follow this third road assume that we can buy just enough "fire insurance" to keep from going to hell. Some believe that a sellout to Jesus in complete, obedient faith is the reserve of a select few who make a "second" decision to make Jesus the Lord of their lives. The problem is we can't *make* Jesus Lord. He is Lord!!

I've heard Jesus presented almost as some kind of divine pizza pie that is cut up into pieces labeled Savior, Lord, Healer, Provider, Friend, etc., as if we are free to chop the Lord of the Universe into bits and respond to one of the bits! This would have been ludicrous to the early disciples. That this point needs to be argued shows how far we have fallen from The Way.

The Lord wants us to present our very bodies as "living sacrifices" which Paul described as our *reasonable* service (Rom. 12:1).

Apparently anything less than such an extreme recognition of our need to give all to Him is not even reasonable.

God wants to fill us with His fire not only so He can "use" us, but so that He can bless us. Here is where our unbelief betrays us. Do we *believe* that His life is superior to our life? Do we *believe* His way is better than ours? Do we trust Him with our whole life?

The Scripture repeatedly describes our God as a loving Father who is kind, patient, faithful, forgiving, merciful, compassionate, holy, gracious, wise and just. Yet many of us expect the worst of Him. Before I understood the true character of God, I inwardly believed that if I really surrendered all to the Lord, He'd test my obedience in some awful way. I pictured Him forcing me to marry a 400-pound, ugly woman and sending me to Africa where I would pine away, dying of malaria, as she smacked me around the mud hut.

If only people knew how good and loving our God is! We should be eager to give the Lord our whole life, gladly presenting ourselves as empty vessels that He can fill up with Himself.

A simple prayer of surrender opens the door for the flame of real zeal to be ignited in our hearts.

> *Breathe on me, Breath of God, fill me with life anew,*
> *That I may love what Thou dost love, and do what*
> *Thou wouldst do.*
> *Breathe on me, Breath of God, until my heart is pure,*
> *Until with Thee I will one will, to do and to endure.*
> *Breathe on me, Breath of God, till I am wholly Thine,*
> *Until this earthly part of me, glows with Thy fire divine.*
> —Hymn by Edwin Hatch and Robert Jackson

Fuel for the fire

There is only one pure fuel for this holy fire. Love for Jesus should be what sparks our zeal and keeps it burning through the years. Like a young man in courtship, that fire within stirs us to do all we can to please and cultivate a relationship with our beloved one. We long to be with Him day and night.

When I first fell in love with my wife, Linda, it was hard for me to think of anything else for several months. When we met, we were both involved in an evangelistic group called "Mission Street Fellowship." As the group's leader, I was careful about how I conducted myself when I was with her. I tried especially hard to maintain a certain reserve and dignity when we were with others. This was spoiled one day when I was descending some steps and noticed Linda walking across the parking lot. I promptly fell down the stairs and landed flat on my face!

As our relationship deepened, I proceeded to do all kinds of things to demonstrate my love for her. I certainly didn't need any outward pressure or law to keep me wooing her. I was stoked on Linda, and I became a man on a mission—to get her to the altar.

Likewise, the more we fall in love with Jesus, the hotter our zeal will be. The apostle Paul, as he was writing to the Corinthians about the need for spiritual zeal in light of eternity, said; "The love of Christ constraineth us…" (2 Cor. 5:14 KJV).

Unfortunately, many Christians think this first-love passion for God is just a passing phase. Certainly, that love fire does cool off in many Christians, but it need not. I have concluded from my experiences and study of Scripture that this passion can actually intensify through the years if we will stoke the flames.

We can stoke our love flame through a continuing quest for intimacy with God and greater acts of devotion (prayer, Bible study, fasting, etc). "And hereby we do know that we know him [Jesus], *if* we keep his commandments. He that saith, I know him, and keepeth not his commandments, is a liar, and the truth is not in him. But whoso keepeth his word, in him verily is the love of God perfected: hereby know we that we are in him. He that saith he abideth in him ought himself also to walk, even as he walked" (1 John 2:3-6 KJV).

Shortly after I made my decision to follow Jesus, I was taught by the "Jesus People" from California's Calvary Chapel that a 100 percent sellout of my life to Jesus was the "normal" Christian life. By committing myself to "actively" love God, I kept from being addicted to the morphine of mediocrity that incapacitates so many new Christians.

A week after my conversion, I was expressing my new-found zeal by passing out Gospel tracts in the produce department of a Safeway store. The management didn't take kindly to my evangelistic fervor and told me so. Ironically, I was consoled by one of "God's little helpers," a girl who was a new Christian herself. Her counsel was: "You have what the Bible calls 'zeal without knowledge.' But don't worry. As you grow in the Lord, you'll mellow out."

The word mellow intrigued me much like the word stoked had earlier. Webster's defines it as "overripe, just about to rot." Shakespeare said, "Prosperity begins to mellow and drop into the rotten mouth of death." Two minutes in the dictionary made me firm in my resolve never to mellow out.

Have you "mellowed out"? Is your Christian life in neutral? Have you allowed yourself, like the proverbial frog in the kettle, to be boiled alive without even knowing it by the rulers of this present darkness? Have you become intoxicated by the obscene materialism, rampant carnality and theological genetic engineering that produces converts who value their biblical rights but not their responsibilities? If you have, or in honesty and humility you must admit you're in danger, turn your heart back to the Lord with new sincerity. He is waiting to embrace you with His love and rekindle your love for Him.

Stoker quote

"I like my tea like I like my religion—boiling hot."

William Booth

Chapter Two

Real Zeal

"He makes winds his messengers, flames of fire his servants."
Psalm 104:4 (NIV)

Bart Starr, quarterback of the former World Champion Green Bay Packers, often speaks of the passion imparted to him by his mentor and coach, Vince Lombardi. "He taught me that you must have a flaming desire to win. It's got to dominate all your waking hours. It's got to glow in you all the time."

Throughout the world of sports, we see this "glow." Gail Devers, who once was within two days of getting both her feet amputated, recovered and went on to win the gold medal in the 100-meter dash at the 1992 Olympics. Despite two earlier failures, Pablo Morales postponed a promising law career to pursue and eventually win a gold medal in swimming at the same Olympics. Similar illustrations can be given from almost every field of human endeavor. A burning passion can raise ordinary people to pinnacles of success.

How about the Christian life? Isn't it logical that we who have God's holy fire in our hearts be even more passionate than an athlete or business executive? After all, we're not just talking about winning a race or scoring some financial gain. The choices we make can affect the eternal destiny of countless others.

How can we be complacent when we see our enemy trying to destroy so many individuals and nations? How can we sit by when we see the unspeakable horrors that sin wreaks in the lives of people all around us? With the stakes this high, we cannot be satisfied with the status quo or some loose, lazy, lukewarm Christianity. Far too many Christians behave like elderly folks sitting at a bus stop waiting for the rapture, rather than like an army of disciplined soldiers who are occupying until the Lord returns.

This is not to say that God will reject us if we don't start marching for Jesus. We must never forget that our salvation is secured by faith—not by our great zeal or works for God. Faith in Christ gives us a position of sonship in God's Kingdom and a guarantee of unconditional love from the Father.

But we must also remember that a father's heart is cultivated by the love and obedience of his children. Our heavenly father has given us not only the privilege of being sons and daughters in His family, but also of standing with Him as a soldier in His army. God's children need to be, "As arrows in the hand of a mighty man" (Ps. 127:4 KJV) to inflict pain into the heart of God's enemies—the forces of darkness who are blinding millions of souls and hundreds of nations to the truth that could set them free. We must allow God to break us, bend us and mold us to be armed and dangerous; lethal weapons in the bow of the Master Archer.

We must not be satisfied until we are characterized by a happy, holy, fervent, fiery zeal that will not burn out until that glorious day when "the kingdoms of this world are become the kingdoms of our Lord, and of his Christ" (Rev. 11:15 KJV).

God's Flamethrowers

In the New Testament, there are two Greek word groups that relate to zeal. One is *zelos* from which we get our English words zeal or jealousy. It means literally "to boil, rage or ferment, to see the with emotion." It refers to an emotion (based on a fervent belief) that leads to action. As Jesus drove out the moneychangers, John 2:17 says He was consumed with *zeal* for His Father's house to the point of it "eating him up."

Paul, while condemning false zeal (Rom. 10:2, Gal. 4:17), wrote much about the merits of spiritual *zelos*. He tells us to be zealous for the Gospel (1 Cor. 14:12) and the welfare of others (Col. 4:13). He even commended the Corinthians for their zealous financial giving that "stirred up many others" (2 Cor. 9:2).

The other word group related to zeal comes from the verb *speudo* from which we get our English words speed or speedy. It means "to be eager, to hasten, to hurry," as in fulfilling a task. It can also describe an inner attitude of eagerness or diligence. Greek scholar W. E. Vine describes it as "zeal and the haste accompanying it." It gives the idea of instant obedience, and being eager to do your best.

Speudo is used to describe the diligence we are to apply in doing business (Rom. 12:11); maintaining unity (Eph. 4:3) and fellowship (1 Thes. 2:17); exercising church discipline (2 Cor. 7:11); helping the poor (Gal. 2:10); leading others (Rom. 12:8); studying the Word (2 Tim. 2:15); and confirming our calling (2 Peter 1:10).

We see from studying these two word groups in their contexts that real zeal is not the reserve of just the emotional, high potency, "type A" personalities among us. It is the inheritance of all of us who call on the name of the Lord. It is easy to see then how Catherine Booth concluded; "Real Christianity is, in its very nature and essence, aggressive."

In Jesus' time, there was a radical sect of the Jews called the Zealots. Founded by Judas of Galilee in AD 6, the Zealots were determined to resist Roman rule and were extremely jealous for God's honor. Their hero in Jewish history was Phinehas, who was credited with stopping the plague of Baal-Peor by making a "spear shish kebab" out of a rebellious Jew and his Midianite girlfriend as they lay together in their tent. Jehovah said of him, "Phinehas,...the priest, has turned my anger away from the Israelites; for he was as zealous as I am for my honor among them, so that in my zeal I did not put an end to them. Therefore tell him I am making my covenant of peace with him. He and his descendants will have a covenant of a lasting priesthood, because he was **zealous** for the honor of his God" (Num. 25:6-15 NIV).

At a time when most Jews passively resisted the oppressive Roman rule, the Zealots put their discontent into action. They organized a formal revolt in AD 66 and fought Rome's invading armies as they destroyed Jerusalem under Titus in AD 70. A band of Zealots under Eleazear Ben Jair fought their last battle at a rock fortress called Massada. Besieged and starved by the Romans, they opted for mass suicide rather than surrender.

From this "stock," Jesus chose one of his Apostles—Simon the Zealot (Luke 6:15). Was this because he knew that the fire in Simon, if transferred from political hatred to spiritual zeal, could be a sparkplug within His apostolic band? In any event, the fact that Jesus chose a Zealot as one of the Twelve indicates He at least wanted to "salt" His team with this religious fervor.

Any "Who's Who" list of Bible heroes will reveal an all-star team of men and women who went to extremes in their zeal for God. The Lord loves all His children, but He seems to have a soft spot in His heart for those whose idea of "balance" was being totally sold out to Him.

Elijah declared that he was "zealous for the Lord God..." shortly after he triumphed over the 450 prophets of Baal (1 Kings 18). Ezekiel laid on his side for 390 days and ate food cooked with dung to illustrate his point to Israel (Ezek. 4:4-15). And how about Hosea, willing to marry a prostitute to help Israel see their spiritual adultery? Or Jeremiah, the weeping prophet, or the psalmist who declared that "streams of tears flow from my eyes, for your law is not obeyed" (Ps. 119:136 NIV).

For honorable mention we could cite John the Baptist, that locust-eating, first century radical who desired more than anything to "decrease that Christ would increase" (John 3:30), and proved it by losing his head! And let's not forget the Sons of Thunder, James and John, who wanted to call down fire from Heaven to consume the Lord's enemies (Luke 9:54).

And then there's Peter. The ol' Rock definitely belongs in the Zealot Hall of Fame. He was the only disciple to venture out of the boat and walk on water (Matt. 14:29). In his zeal to protect Jesus he did an ear-amputation on a Roman guard named Malchus (John 18:10). The Bible's various accounts of Peter point out many failings, but Peter could never be accused of being lukewarm. Years after his time with Jesus, Peter prophetically described the fiery end of the world and challenged us:

> *"Therefore, beloved, since you wait for these, be*
> ***zealous*** *to be found by him without spot or blemish,*
> *and at peace"* (2 Pet. 3:14 KJV).

Divine "Insanity"

The above accounts of God's "extremists" cause us to ponder an important principle as we seek to blaze ahead for the Lord. It is summed up in a statement Paul made to the Christians living among the intellectual, skeptical Greeks at Corinth; "The message of the cross is foolishness to those who are perishing..." (1 Cor. 1:18 NKJV).

The Greek word translated here as foolishness is *moria* from which we get our word moron. What Paul is saying is that the message we preach and the lifestyle we live are viewed as absurd to the unbelievers, and our moronic appearance will intensify the more on-fire for God we become.

When a once-respected Pharisee, Paul, gave his testimony before King Agrippa he was accused of being "mad," when in fact, Paul viewed his former lifestyle as madness and his present belief as "truth and soberness" (Acts 26:11,24,25). Jesus himself was accused by both his friends and enemies of being "beside himself," and by others that He was demonized (Mark 3:21). Jeremiah, Hosea and others were thought to be out of their minds.

In more recent history, other "crazies" have accomplished great things for the Kingdom of God. A young couple named William and Catherine Booth were appalled by the conditions of poverty, alcoholism and despair in London and formed the Salvation Army in 1865. Many thought them crazy for giving up their lives to serve the destitute masses, but their ministry set 70 nations ablaze in just 30 years!

John Wesley, who described himself as "a brand plucked from the burning," tirelessly preached from town to town throughout England. His flaming zeal for Christ set thousands of other "Methodists" on fire and many fanned out around the world with the Gospel. Wesley was happily stoked on Jesus.

One legend about the great English preacher's zeal is a story about him riding in a carriage on his way to give a commencement speech at a university. Near his destination, he noticed a funeral procession. He suddenly leaped from the carriage, ran to the grave site, delivered a Gospel message, invited the mourners to receive Christ, and then ran to the university in time to deliver his message to the graduates.

Wesley was so zealous about the use of his time that he scheduled his days into five-minute increments to minimize wasted time.[1] His Methodist followers (so named because of their methods of spiritual discipline) carried on the zealous lifestyle that first caught fire in their leader's heart.

One of the most stoked of all Christians was American Dwight L. Moody. Before his conversion, the Chicago shoe salesman's goal in life was to make $100,000. But Jesus set his heart on fire. He came to be known in the press as "Crazy Moody" because of his incessant street witnessing, door-to-door visitation, and transporting kids to Sunday School on his "missionary horse." His uncle once told an interviewer, "My nephew Dwight is crazy—crazy as a March Hare."

Without formal education, Moody founded three schools that trained hundreds of ministers. Lacking experience in journalism didn't keep him from founding two of America's largest publishing houses, Fleming Revell and Moody Press. He pioneered Sunday School work among the poor, changed the face of mass evangelism,

---

1. J. O. Sanders, *Spiritual Leadership* (Chicago: Moody Press) 119.

travelled over one million miles to preach to over 100 million people, and depopulated hell by nearly a million souls. If this is crazy, we need all the crazy people we can get!

Moody said of himself: "I suppose they say of me, 'He is a radical; he is a fanatic; he only has one idea.' Well, it is a glorious idea. I would rather have that said of me than be a man of ten thousand ideas and do nothing with them. The world has yet to see what God can do with a man fully consecrated to Him. By God's grace, I aim to be that man."[2]

---

2. *Christian History* Magazine, Issue 25.

Stoker quote

"If God should ask you this moment, by an audible voice from heaven, 'Do you want a revival?' would you dare say Yes? Are you willing to make the sacrifices? Would you answer 'Yes! Let it begin tonight—let it begin here—let it begin in my heart?'"

Charles Finney

Chapter Three

Fire in the Circle

*"I have come to set fire to the earth, and
how I wish it were already kindled!"*
Luke 12:49 (NEB)

Gypsy Smith, the fiery British evangelist,
was once asked by a woman how to promote a revival and how to
recognize it once it came. Without flinching, Smith instructed her
to buy a piece of chalk and take it home with her. He then told her
to find a quiet place in her home and draw a large circle on the
floor around herself. "After you've drawn the circle, get on your
knees inside it and cry out to God for revival to break out in the
middle of the circle. When He answers that prayer, you've got
revival!"

What Smith was saying, in a creative way, was that revival
begins with us individually. Revival fire must first burn in us before
it can have an effect on the world.

"If *my* people, which are called by my name, shall humble themselves, and pray...then will I hear from heaven, and will forgive their

sin, and will heal their land" (2 Chron. 7:14 KJV). Revival first comes to God's people. Revival is a new beginning—something that had died and now is alive again. The world doesn't need to be revived, but "vived." It is *we* who need to be revived. Unfortunately, those of us who think we need it least, need it most.

Revival is not a series of high-powered meetings where a hyper-active evangelist keeps the hell-bound spell-bound. It doesn't begin with drug addicts burning their syringes or alcoholics going straight. It's not kicking all the secular humanists out of Congress and electing a born-again President. Those things may be the fruits of revival but are not its root. Revival begins quietly, deep in the innermost being of the "revivable" Christian. That person has made himself a candidate by calling out to God from inside "the circle."

How about you? Are you revivable? Are you "in the circle"? Do you see the desperate need that you have to be broken at the foot of the cross, humbly confessing your need for a fresh fire to burn in your soul? It must start there. You must not make the fatal mistake of the Pharisee who thanked God that he was not like the repentant tax collector. But like the tax collector you must beat *your* breast and ask God's mercy on *you* (Luke 18:9-14).

Jesus put personal revival in simple terms when He affirmed the Old Testament's two great commandments: "Thou shalt love the Lord thy God with all thine heart...soul...and might" (Deut. 6:5 KJV) and "love thy neighbour as thyself" (Lev. 19:18 KJV). In emphasizing these directives, Jesus drew attention to the distinct ways we can love God and our neighbor: with our heart, our soul, and our strength. Let's take revival out of the "ozone" and bring it down to the same simple terms. To make ourselves revivable, we only have to love God and our neighbor completely. If you're doing that, consider yourself revived!

Revival in the Heart

The first area Jesus zeroes in on is the heart. The heart in the Bible is simply your innermost being. It is the "cockpit" of your life, from where you make your ultimate choices concerning what you will direct your soul, mind and strength to do. Your heart is the real you. The Bible says we can have a pure, good, humble, true, large and burning heart. It also says our heart can be hard, foolish, evil, blind, deceived, condemned and even satanic.[1]

The choice is ours. Jesus said, "A good man out of the good treasure of the heart bringeth forth good things: and an evil man out of the evil treasure bringeth forth evil things" (Matt. 12:35 KJV), and that "Where your treasure is, there will your heart be also" (Matt. 6:21 KJV). In other words, your outward actions reflect what's in your heart. Are you doing evil things? Then your heart is evil. Are you doing good things? Then your heart is good. Is your treasure (money) wrapped up in this world? Then that's where your heart is. The condition of your heart is the bottom line on success or failure in the Christian life.

One of the maladies that afflicts Christians is the "divided" heart. Even David needed to pray that God would "unite" his heart, as if he had cardiac schizophrenia (Ps. 86:11). Paul the Apostle seemed to have the same problem (Rom. 7). He wanted to do good, but evil often got the upper hand in his life.

So what's a guy to do? Well, consider the old spiritual illustration of the two dogs, a black one and a white one, that fight constantly. The one you feed the most is the one that wins the fight!

We have two warring forces inside us—the carnal, Adam-nature we call the flesh, and the new man, regenerated by the Spirit of God. "He who sows to the flesh will of the flesh reap corruption, but he who sows to the Spirit will...reap everlasting life" (Gal. 6:8 NKJV). Here lies the issue: where and to what will we choose to "sow" our seeds? Which dog are we feeding? The answer lies deep within the heart. Being stoked or unstoked is totally dependent on the condition of the heart. Solomon told us, "Above all else, guard your heart, for it is the wellspring of life" (Prov. 4:23 NIV).

The Bible uses the word heart over a thousand times. Most of these references are not about the blood pump within our chests. They focus on what we call the will. Scripture clearly implies that

---

1. Matt. 5:8; Luke 8:15; Matt. 11:29; Heb. 10:22; 2 Cor. 6:11; Luke 24:32; Rom. 1:21, 2:5; Matt. 13:15; Heb. 3:12; Eph. 4:18; Jas. 1:26; 1 John 3:20; Acts 5:3.

we have a free will because we are implored hundreds of times to obey God. However, true revival is not just acting in cold obedience to a set of commandments, but "...doing the will of God from the heart" (Eph. 6:6 KJV).

Evangelist Leonard Ravenhill once said, "The reason we don't have revival is because we're content to live without it." While we can't revive ourselves by chest-thumping willpower or positive confessions, we can cry out to God like David; "Create in me a clean heart, O God..." (Ps. 51:10 KJV), and by an act of will make ourselves "stokable."

The most effective way to win the "civil war" in our hearts is to put down the rebel forces by a constant diet of God's Word. Our hearts by nature are "deceitful...and desperately wicked..." (Jer. 17:9 KJV). Therefore, we need the two-edged sword of God's Word to cut the fine line in us between soul and spirit and help us to judge the "thoughts and intentions of the heart" (Heb. 4:12 RSV).

It was as Jesus was opening the Scriptures to the disciples on Emmaus road that their hearts "burned within them" (Luke 24:32). When we unite our faith with the truths of God's Word our divided heart is united and set ablaze. This new heart then steers our life down the narrow road of glory. Therefore, let us pray as David did: "Give me an undivided heart, that I may fear your name" (Ps. 86:11 NIV).

Revival in the Soul

"Wilt thou not revive us again: that thy people may rejoice in thee?" (Ps. 85:6 KJV)

While revival does not begin in the emotions, our feelings should definitely reap the benefits of a heart that is blazing for God. Your soul in essence is the seat of your personality, pathos and passion. And your body expresses what's in your soul.

Some cultures are wide open to expressions of the soul, while others sometimes miss God's blessing by resisting them. Living in Honolulu, I've delighted in the vibrant, expressive worship of my Pacific Island brothers and sisters. Another example is in the

African-American culture, which many describe as possessing "soul." Try listening to some southern black Gospel music and not be moved in your soul.

Once when I was a fairly new Christian, I visited a small Pentecostal church in California. With shoulder-length hair and bib-overalls, I must have looked like quite a free spirit to the elderly saints who had gathered for worship that summer evening. But it was they who taught me how to be free in the spirit.

Being rather sheepish as a new convert and a bit stoic in personality, I clapped my hands softly and lifted my arms at "half-mast" during worship. Brother Weaver, an elderly man who still had the "glory glow" on his face from the 1904 Azusa Street revival, shuffled over to me. With a love and authority that seemed to come directly from the Throne of God, he said, "Don't fight the feelin', brother. Let it go. Get into it. God ain't nervous!"

Since then, I have tried not to "fight the feelin'." I want to let loose with the emotions that God gave me as a part of my being. Few things are more pitiful than a cerebral, feelingless, dead orthodoxy that makes Christians look like they're being baptized in lemon juice rather than living water. I've been in churches that were so cold you felt like you could ice skate down the aisles!

Many folks feel that we must act dignified in church because we're in the presence of Deity. But God doesn't just abide in church sanctuaries. We're in the presence of the Deity all the time! I don't believe the Lord is pleased with all the stuffed-shirt religion that is defined as dignified worship. Who says a church service should resemble a funeral? We are God's chosen people, not his frozen people!

The Greek word translated as "soul" in the Bible, *psuche*, is also rendered as "life" in some places. A truly stoked heart will elicit life—life that will affect every part of your being, including your feelings.

William T. Stead, the London editor of the *Pall Mall Gazette*, visited the Welsh Revival in 1905. His observation; "It is a very real thing, this revival, a live thing which seems to have a power and a grip...it is like a revolution and is apt to be wonderfully catching.

There is something there from the other world. You cannot say [from] whence it came or whither it is going, but it lives and moves and reaches for you all the time."[2]

Revival means new life, and it's a life that changes things.

A. W. Tozer once said, "God dwells in a state of perpetual enthusiasm." The English word enthusiasm comes from the Greek words *en* (in) and *Theos* (God). So if we are "in God" we should be enthusiastic about it! After all, our sins are forgiven, all guilt is gone, our bodies are the dwelling place of God. We have His love, joy, peace, friendship and have heaven guaranteed as our eternal home. We should be stoked!

This joyful enthusiasm seems to be the norm among many godly people in the Bible. David sure didn't "fight the feelin' " when he donned his linen ephod and danced before the Ark of the Covenant (2 Sam. 6:14). In the Psalm 47, he exhorted us to "...clap your hands, shout to God with a voice of triumph..."

In our society, we'll go wild with enthusiasm at a football game, a prizefight, a political rally or a rock concert. Yet when we stand before the Creator of the Universe and Redeemer of our souls, many of us resemble a morgue more than a many-membered Body alive and vibrant with divine energy. In no way is that God's intent!

One of the first "fruits" to look for after the "root" of revival has taken hold is joy. The psalmist prayed for revival so the people could experience the joy of the Lord, "In thy presence is fullness of joy" (Ps. 16:11 KJV). A joyful life is evidence that the Spirit is reigning in us (Gal. 5:22). The Bible is full of promises that it is God's will for us to be fueled with joy.

Many recent moves of the Holy Spirit throughout the world have been characterized by joy. It is a strong antidote to the hopelessness and depression that have so infected our society. Since "the joy of the Lord is your strength" (Neh. 8:10 KJV), it's no wonder that Satan tries so hard to rob us of joy.

A few summers ago, I went through a particularly trying time. It seemed as if some crazed telephone operator had given my number

---

2. Winkey Pratney, *Revival* (Whitaker House, 1984) 193.

to every weird bird and false prophet under the sun. One woman prophesied my apostasy from the faith, and that my family would follow me into the pit. Another said the Lord showed him a dream that my wife would divorce me. Another said God had written Ichabod ("The glory has departed") over the door of my ministry. Then to top it off, one disillusioned "seer" said God showed him I was using mind-control techniques to direct the lives of young missionaries, and that I was in Youth With A Mission for the money.

Those last accusations clearly showed that he was deceived. Anyone who knows me, knows I'm barely smart enough to control my own mind much less other peoples', and being in YWAM for the money—gimme a break! All of us serving on staff with YWAM are unpaid volunteers who must raise our own personal support. Looking back, these accusations seem bizarre. But at the time, they caused me to question my faith and integrity, and they started sapping my joy and zeal.

Even though I was counseled by my leadership team to ignore these false charges, they continued to trouble me. Then one day while shaving, with my eyebrows burrowed in serious introspection, I asked myself, "Are you, Danny Lehmann, an apostate, greedy, deceiver who is guilty of mind control?" The immediate response, which was intensified by the silly, ultra-serious look on my lathered face was to break out in side-splitting laughter. It was as if God Himself slapped me on my back and let me get in on the belly-laugh He was having. The enemy was after my joy, but the Lord didn't let him get it. "He who sits in the heavens shall laugh" (Ps. 2:4 NKJV).

I believe one of the most effective weapons in spiritual warfare is a good sense of humor, especially the ability to laugh at yourself. This is a part of what it means to be childlike. A child doesn't worry much about the crime rate, the high cost of living, whether he'll impress the movers and shakers at a "power lunch," or whether his cholesterol is over 200. Children get up every day, throw on some clothes (caring little if they match), eat breakfast and take life as it comes. They live life to the max and have a blast doing it. We need to make a practice of casting our cares on Jesus and living with a childlike spirit.

Over the years, I've tried to keep from taking myself too seriously. We preachers deal with eternal issues like heaven and hell, life and death, etc. on a daily basis—so we need regular doses of humor and joy. Proverbs 16:24 (NAS) says, "Pleasant words [I believe this includes humor] are a honeycomb, sweet to the soul and healing to the bones." It's just plain healthy for us "serious" Christians to "lighten up."

One thing I've *had* to laugh about is my squeaky preaching voice. Being a street evangelist, I am almost embarrassed by its volume. Usually I can't be heard much more than a stone's throw away, and my volume gets weaker the longer I preach. I was once told that after about 15 minutes of high-pitched street sermonizing, I sounded like Pinocchio's Jiminy Cricket at double-speed. Another heckler likened me to one of Alvin's chipmunks. I can laugh too because even though I don't possess a great oratory instrument, God has used the one I have to draw many people to Christ.

A veteran missionary once told me that two things were necessary if you wanted to be happy in foreign missionary work: a good sense of humor and no sense of smell!

One great example is a Swedish missionary. When some friends tried to dissuade him from returning to India in summer because it was 120 degrees in the shade, he replied: "Vell, ve don't have to stay in the shade, do ve?"

When the Lord commands us to rejoice in all circumstances, He does not want us to redouble our intensity or crank up our willpower. He simply wants us to *choose* to be joyful in Him. Brent Chambers of Scripture In Song once wrote a worship song called "I Will Rejoice" that says it all:

> *It doesn't depend on my circumstance*
> *The strength of my heart or my voice*
> *It doesn't depend on the way I feel*
> *I've made up my mind that I'm gonna rejoice*
> *I will rejoice, I will rejoice, I will rejoice*
> *For I've made my choice to rejoice in the Lord*

Revival of Strength (Physical Fire)

What does it mean to love God with all our strength? There are two good answers. Jesus may have been referring to an all-out physical expression of our love for God. Or He could have been commanding maximum physical effort in the combined areas of heart, soul and mind. Either way, the mention of the word "all" four times in the text suggests we need an all-out, go-for-broke attitude in our efforts to seek and serve the Lord.

Jacob displayed that attitude in his relentless pursuit of God's blessing. He used all his strength in his all-night wrestling match with an angel. And he wouldn't release his grip until the angel blessed him (Gen. 32:24-29). Are we willing to expend that kind of effort to win God's blessing, or to present the good news of Jesus to a lost world?

Once a young applicant for the U.S. nuclear submarine program had an interview with the formidable Admiral Hyman Rickover. When asked about his qualifications for the job, the young man swelled his chest and proudly declared he had graduated 59th out of a class of 820 at the U.S. Naval Academy. As the applicant waited for some sign of affirmation, the Admiral looked up and asked, "Did you do your best?" He started to say, "Yes, sir," but remembered many times when he had sloughed off and admitted, "No, sir, I didn't always do my best."

Rickover turned his chair around and finished the interview with a two-word question: "Why not?" Future U.S. President Jimmy Carter left the room shaken, but he never forgot the admiral's question. Years later, he wrote a book entitled, *Why Not the Best?* in which he told how this experience made him dedicated to excellence.

Does not the Creator of the Universe and lover of our souls deserve "the best" from us? Several books on management stress the importance of pursuing excellence in producing a product, procuring a sale or servicing a customer's needs. Should we not give God all our strength in order to present to Him a "most excellent" vessel for Him to fill with His glory?

To love Him with all our strength and love our neighbors as ourselves requires us to take action. This kind of love has many expressions—like travailing in prayer and fasting; losing sleep to care for a sick or anguished friend; walking the streets to share the love of Jesus; or cleaning up a yard or house for an overwhelmed single parent. Such actions often leave us physically spent, but God doesn't intend to burn us out.

Good theology and common sense tell us that the care and maintenance of our bodies is not only good stewardship of a precious gift God has given us, but is actually a spiritual undertaking. If we believe that our health not only plays a factor, but is essential for us to carry out God's destiny for our lives, we will discipline ourselves to take care of it.

I was recently counseling with another leader about the dangers of burning out instead of burning on for the Lord. While he was telling me he was too busy to exercise or watch his diet, it occurred to him that I was just as busy, if not busier than he was. He then asked how I found time to go running five or six days a week. I said, "I came to a point in my life that I became convinced it was God's will that I run, not just as an activity that relieves stress, but as part of His intention for me."

Consequently, when someone asks if I'm busy during a period of time when I have a workout scheduled, without a shred of guilt, I'll answer "yes." I have found that if you are not as rigid with physical exercise as you are with the other spiritual disciplines of Bible study, prayer, fasting, solitude and rest, then something will always come up that will rob you of that which will enable you to better "...glorify God in your body, and your spirit, which are God's" (1 Cor. 6:20 KJV).

Seeing the power of God at work in our "earthly vessels" is often one of the greatest testimonies of His mighty power.

Over the years, millions were in awe of Mother Teresa. They wondered how that frail, elderly woman could keep pouring her life out for the poor in the wretched slums of Calcutta, India. There is only one answer: Jesus. He renewed her strength so she could run and not be weary (Isa. 40:31).

Dwight Moody, the great 19th century Chicago evangelist, poured out his strength in a similar way through his relentless evangelism and service to the needy. His brother once said: "Dwight is running from morning to night. He hardly gets time to eat." But Moody kept on going, and eventually won the admiration of many who once thought him crazy.

The secret of renewal for Moody and others who are stoked on Jesus is in taking advantage of God's great anti-burnout weapon— the Sabbath. God knew that if we were working diligently and living an on-fire spiritual life that we'd need a weekly day of rest. That's why He repeated the command of Sabbath rest again and again in Scripture.[3]

It's interesting that in Isaiah 58, God promises that if we delight in His Sabbath, He will feed us with the heritage of "our father" Jacob. Yes, we'll be refreshed and renewed just like that great angel wrestler, who fought with all his might to win the blessing of God.

---

3. Danny Lehmann, *Before You Hit the Wall* (YWAM Publishing) 97-107.

Stoker quote

"While women weep as they do now, I'll fight; while little children go hungry as they do now, I'll fight; while men go to prison, in and out, in and out, as they do now, I'll fight—I'll fight to the very end!"
William Booth

Chapter Four

Firefighting—
The Battle for the Mind

"...Be renewed in the spirit of your mind."
Eph. 4:23 (KJV)

The realm of the mind is seldom considered in discussions about revival, but to be revived, our minds must be transformed, too. Jesus said to love the Lord with all our heart, soul, strength—and *mind* (Matt. 22:37-39). A revived Christian is one whose mind is filled with thoughts about God's Word, character and creation. He/she is dedicated to learning not just about the acts of God, but also gaining understanding of His ways and precepts (Ps. 103:7).

Of course, the Lord does not want our spiritual life to be merely an intellectual quest. Jesus castigated the scribes and Pharisees for knowing all about God's law, but missing the heart of it. Unfortunately, there are still many who study about God for years, but let their love for Him wane and sometimes die out altogether. Nowhere in the Scripture does it exhort us to become theological eggheads who walk around with our heads in the clouds. Loving

God with our minds should compliment our love for Him in heart, soul and strength.

On the other side of the pendulum are Christians who consider the mind inherently evil and presuppose a spirituality that comes at the expense of an intellect.

I was led to Christ by a group of people who believed in a strong separation between the human spirit and the human soul. Their reasoning went something like this: The mind is bad because it's carnal. The spirit is good because it's spiritual. Since the mind is part of the soul, its only use is in "soulish" pursuits, such as your occupation, friendships and other natural activities. In other words, your normal everyday life is divorced from your relationship with God, which was to be controlled by your spirit.

Consequently, Bible study was replaced by "pray reading" the Scriptures in a repetitive chant (i.e. John 3:16 for 20 minutes straight), and conversational prayer was replaced by chanting the name of the Lord (O Lord Jesus, O Lord Jesus...). This was intended to "release" your spirit from the shackles of the soul. It didn't take me long to figure out that this was bad theology.

Within a week of this mindless chanting, I was ready to defect to the Hare Krishnas. I figured that if I chanted with them, they'd at least give me some organic vegetarian meals as a bonus! It was then I ran into some folks from the Jesus People revival in Southern California. They set me straight, showing me from the Bible that not only could my mind be renewed (Rom. 12:2), but I was commanded by Jesus to love God with *all* my mind. After four and a half years of drug abuse, "all" was not much, but I was determined to love Him with all of it.

Paul tells us that to be "spiritually minded is life and peace" (Rom. 8:6 KJV). Following are some steps toward becoming spiritually minded:

(1) REPENT

"Repent and be converted..." Acts 3:19 (KJV)

To repent literally means "to change the mind." We tend to see repentance as primarily a message for the lost, but it is also the number one prerequisite for a Christian who wants to be on fire for God. The churches in John's Revelation needed to hear about repentance as did many of the recipients of Paul's letters. An attitude of brokenness, humility and teachability that is quick to change the mind will always be met with God's favor.

Repent is the first word of the Gospel (Mark 1:15), and it should be on the top of our list as a condition of ongoing discipleship. Whether we're eight or 80, a baby or a bishop, a neophyte or a nation changer, we must have a posture that God is wholly right and I am wholly wrong on any subject, and be willing to change as His Spirit convicts us (John 16:8).

One of the most powerful weapons against self-centered carnality and pride is the testimony of a clear conscience (1 Tim. 1:5, 19). The word conscience means "with knowledge." We must keep "short accounts" with the Lord about any bad actions, attitudes or attributes that will douse the flame in our hearts.

(2) RENEW

> *"And do not be conformed to this world, but be*
> *transformed by the renewing of your mind…"*
> Rom. 12:2 (NAS)

After repentance, we can begin renewing our minds. As we read, study, meditate, memorize and hear God's Word being taught, we will have our minds renewed and have more artillery to fight the battle of the mind.[1] We also need to be careful that we monitor what other things go into our minds so they don't subtly conform us to the world's standards. The J.B. Phillips translation of Romans 12:2 reads, "Don't let the world around you squeeze you into its own mold."

Even people who know the Scriptures can fall into this trap. I recently had to correct a Bible teacher who had taken legal action against his Christian landlord in a rental dispute. When I showed him the clear teaching of 1 Corinthians 6 on the subject, he repented and stopped the litigation. He had allowed his mind to be

---

1. Danny Lehmann, *Before You Hit The Wall* (YWAM Publishing) 51-76

squeezed into the world's mold. For him, the renewal process not only included repentance, but actions that confirmed his obedience to God's Word. As he did so, the Lord soon worked out the problem.

I am a strong advocate of Scripture memorization for many reasons, not the least of which is that it keeps the mental muscle exercised while renewing our minds with God's truth. Jesus said, "You will know the truth and the truth will set you free" (John 8:32 PHILLIPS). The more of God's truth you know and act upon, the more capacity you have to be free, not only from sin and Satan but from the kind of worldly thinking that brings bondage.

If you're a man and are being pressured to value a "macho" image or to strive after riches, let God's Word renew you by saturating your mind with the truth about what it means to be a godly man. If you're a woman bombarded with worldly temptations to dress and act like a "Vogue" woman, meditate on God's design for women in Proverbs 31. If you're a young person under peer pressure to have sex or do drugs, follow Paul's example to consider other peoples' opinions a "very small thing" (1 Cor. 4:3-4).

(3) REPROGRAM

> "...whatever is true, whatever is honorable, whatever is right, whatever is pure, whatever is lovely, whatever is of good report,...dwell on these things" Phil. 4:8 (NAS).

It takes an act of our will to reprogram our minds. Much like a computer, our mind responds based on what we put in it. We reprogram our mind by supplanting old "data" with new positive thoughts based on Jesus. Notice that the six things listed in the verse above are positive, and each could be applied to the Lord Jesus Himself.

I was at a church recently that had been in the throes of the controversial "word-faith" teaching. I had mentioned something about positive thinking in my message and was angrily confronted by a woman afterward. "You're into the positive confession, 'name it-claim it' doctrine, aren't you?" I assured her I wasn't, but then I responded, "I'm not into the negative confession doctrine either!" I went on to explain that, while we must be wary of erroneous teaching, we must be careful not to throw the baby out with the bathwater. God is *the* eternal optimist. Nothing is impossible to Him (Luke 1:37). For Him to part the Red Sea, raise Jesus from the dead or take losers like us and empower us to evangelize the world requires optimism.

There is no power in positive thinking, per se, but there is power in believing God and His ability to keep His Word. Hence we need to think on whatever is:

> **True**—Do you rely on the truth of God's Word or live by the standards of our culture?
>
> **Honorable**—Do you honor heroes with moral courage or the cynical "tabloid" heroes of the world?
>
> **Just**—Are your concepts of justice based on the Bible or on the ever-changing world standards of "fairness?"
>
> **Pure**—Do you value moral and sexual purity or accept non-traditional sexual relationships as OK?
>
> **Lovely**—Are you spending as much time appreciating the beauty of creation as you are watching violent TV shows and movies?
>
> **Good Report**—Are you spreading positive comments about people or gossip and slander?

There's a 19th century proverb that says, "Sow a thought, reap an action. Sow an action, reap a habit. Sow a habit, reap a character. Sow a character, reap a destiny."

Since our ultimate destiny may be determined by our thoughts, we should be careful what we bring into our minds. Guarding our minds is not easy in this information age. Advertising experts estimate that our minds are bombarded with approximately 1,800 "sales pitches" every day through signs, billboards, bumper stickers, newspapers, magazines, radio, television and other media. Many of us worsen the problem by devoting ourselves to worldly amusements that deaden our hearts and minds.

The psalmist writes: "My heart was hot within me; while I was musing the fire burned" (Ps. 39:3 NAS). In this text, the word "muse" means to meditate or concentrate. This is where we get the word music. An "a-musement" comes from a word which means "not to think" or "no-musing." We should be on our guard lest we spend too much time in amusements that let our mental muscles go flabby.

Exercising our minds takes much the same kind of discipline and concentration as exercising the physical body. We build our minds up with a steady diet of true, honorable, just, pure, lovely and admirable things. As we do, we'll see our actions, habits, character and destiny change before our eyes. The mind that is empowered and quickened by God's Spirit becomes a mighty weapon for defending against and casting down Satanic thoughts.

God wants us to use this weapon in the great battle for our souls that is raging on Earth and in the Heavenlies. He calls on us to begin by pulling down satanic strongholds in our minds. "Casting down imaginations, and every high thing that exalteth itself against the knowledge of God, and bringing into captivity *every thought* to the obedience of Christ" (2 Cor. 10:5 KJV).

The Great Battleground

As a new believer witnessing on the streets of a university town, I encountered intellectual skeptics almost daily. Some asked odd questions about things like the fate of the pygmies in Africa or where Cain got his wife. But others plagued me with tough questions on the existence of God, the uniqueness of Christ, divine inspiration of the Bible, the Resurrection and a host of other issues. My first response was a "God said it, I believe it, that settles it" attitude. I didn't try to defend the truth because the truth defends itself, or so I thought.

Then I discovered that not only in the Bible, but in church history, God has raised up people to "think Christian-ly" and confront unbelief and skepticism head on by giving to "every man an answer." The word for "answer" in 1 Peter. 3:15 is *apologia* which means to give "a rational defense" for the Gospel. Paul declared he was "set for the defense of the Gospel" (Phil. 1:7, 17 KJV) and Jude tells us to "earnestly contend for the faith." This "contending for the faith" requires that we do the study necessary to give honest answers to the honest questions of our generation.

We are in a battle for the minds of millions, and the only ideas that are life-giving are God's ideas. The battle line today centers on the "worldview" or the thinking processes of the masses. Whether we recognize it or not, most people ascribe to some worldview—be it Christian, Muslim, Humanist, Marxist, New Age or whatever. Many seek to shape the way people think, recognizing that if you influence their thoughts, you also influence their actions.

That's why it's so important for Christians to make sure our values are solidly based on Biblical truth rather than other views.

One current example of how a non-Christian worldview has slowly influenced many Christians and the nation itself is the issue of abortion. Only a generation ago abortion was viewed as murder by most Americans, but now it is widely seen as a "right of choice" for women. Why? Because powerful people with a Humanist worldview have been working to turn our nation's thinking. If they prevail, in a few years it may be considered a "good moral choice" to abort a baby so that medical experiments can be done on its tissues.

The Lord invites us to test His ideas and "reason together" with Him (Isa. 1:18). He loves it when we seek to know Him and understand His ways (Jer. 9:24). Solomon urged us to "cry out for insight and cry aloud for understanding" and to "look for it as for silver and search for it as for hidden treasure" (Prov. 2:3-4 NIV). Paul prayed for the Ephesians that the "eyes of their understanding" (Eph.1:18) would be opened.

So what does this have to do with zeal and being stoked on Jesus? Simply this: Our zeal needs to be focused in the right direction. Misdirected zeal can be worse than no zeal at all. Paul accused the Jews of having "zeal without knowledge" (Rom. 10:2). We don't want to be like the Jewish marathoner Ahimaaz who was so excited to give King David a message that he overran another messenger named Cushi. When he got to David, he realized he didn't know what the message was! (2 Samuel 18:19-33)

A Holy "Tick Off" in the House of God

"While Paul was waiting for them in Athens, he was greatly distressed to see that the city was full of idols" Acts 17:16 (NIV).

Although it may sound like a strange characteristic of revival, righteous anger is a highly combustible fuel to keep our hearts aflame for God. In the above passage, the word translated "greatly distressed" literally means "to become enraged." Paul was enraged that Athens was full of idols. This anger and "distress" led him to enter the synagogue and preach the Gospel.

This "positive" anger is described in Mark 3:5 when Jesus "looked on them with anger." In another instance, anger was His way of expressing His zeal for the House of God (John 2:15-17). Psalm 7:11 (NIV) says, "God is angry with the wicked every day." Many other Scripture passages speak of the wrath of a just and holy (and I might add, *loving*) God.

Christians don't usually think of anger in a positive light because most of the anger we see today is sin. Both slow seething anger and angry outbursts are condemned by the Apostle Paul as works of the flesh. But while warning us to avoid the sin of anger, the Bible *commands* us to be angry (Eph. 4:26) in other instances.

Anger is a God-given emotion that if channeled in the right way at the right time can achieve much good. But unlike human anger, God's anger is always under control and always balanced with mercy and compassion. It is a strong motivator for action from a truly stoked heart. About what then are we to be angry? In general, we should be angry at anything that God is angry at. Here are some specifics:

We should be angry at sin and the pain it causes —Acts 17:16

Sin causes untold hurt and pain to millions, and breaks the heart of a loving heavenly Father. Anger and hatred for sin, combined with love for God, create a strong basis for action.

I have a friend named Marty Huber who went on a short-term outreach to Manila's infamous Smokey Mountain garbage dump. One day, he was asked to care for a malnourished baby boy while his mother went out to scavenge behind the returning garbage trucks. To his horror, the baby died in his arms before the mother came back. A torrent of emotions welled up in his soul. One hot emotion was anger over the squalid conditions that caused people to live in such misery.

Marty's anger motivated him to go to the United States, get some medical training, and return to Smokey Mountain to help the people there. By God's grace, Marty has seen many souls saved, bodies healed, enemies reconciled, and a church planted at Smokey Mountain. He also has worked with the Philippine government to improve the living conditions on the dump. He was righteously "ticked off" and it bore good fruit for God's Kingdom.

We should be angry at Satan and the powers of darkness.

I used to think I could make some kind of deal with the devil. I figured if I left him alone he would leave me alone. I found out, of course, that he doesn't make those kinds of deals.

As we view with horror (Ps. 119:53) the increasingly wicked conditions in the world, we need to recognize their origin. Satan's ongoing rebellion against God continues to wreak havoc on individuals and society. Acting under his influence, people increase in their lawlessness, and the result is a moral landslide of filth, selfishness, oppression of the poor and thousands of other miseries. They cause millions of broken hearts, not only in time, but in eternity. We should hate the devil and his demons, not only because of their rebellion against the Lord, but because of their destructive influence on so many lives.

Martin Luther gave us a good example of devil-directed anger when he threw his inkwell at the Prince of Darkness when he appeared in his doorway one day. Luther often said he did his best work for God when he was angry. His anger was aimed in the right direction as he, with his preaching and writing, attacked a religious system that was deceiving millions as to the way of salvation. In a marketplace in Wittenberg, Germany, Luther saw a religious leader selling pardons for sin and was outraged that the church had stooped to such depths. Luther knew from the Bible that "The just shall live by faith" (Rom. 1:17 KJV). He proceeded to write out 95 theses in protest and nailed them on the door of the church. The Reformation was born and the course of history changed.

We should be angry at hypocrisy in the church.

Jesus was so angry over the misuse of His Father's House that He drove the money changers out of the temple (John 2:15-17). We know it wasn't just an outburst of anger because He apparently took the time to make a scourge of cords. His anger was directed at the "religious" sinners who should have known better. You can sense the heat of His anger against the Pharisees when, among other things, He accused them of being hell-bound serpents and vipers (Matt. 23).

I believe Jesus gives us a portion of His own righteous anger so we can speak out against religious hypocrisy when we see it. We should be outraged when we see charlatans making a circus out of the Gospel of Jesus Christ. We should be angry when God's precious sheep are led astray by pastors or teachers who don't practice what they preach. It should sicken us to see people profess to know God but deny Him by their works (Titus 1:16).

In recent decades, "angry men" such as A.W. Tozer, Leonard Ravenhill, Keith Green, David Wilkerson and others have continued to speak out prophetically against hypocrisy in the church. It would serve us well to periodically feel the heat of God's anger as expressed through such prophetic voices. God wants us to be stoked with the same passion for keeping His church holy and blameless in a perverse generation.

Stoker quote

"*In many instances, ministerial success is traceable almost entirely to an intense zeal, a consuming passion for souls and an eager enthusiasm in the cause of God. Men prosper in the Divine service in proportion as their hearts are blazing with Holy love.*"

Charles Spurgeon

Chapter Five

Holy Fire

"Without holiness, no one shall see the Lord."
Hebrews 12:14 (NIV)

"Danny, I'm dying. Can you come see me?" The raspy voice of my friend Larry, a former co-worker in the Gospel, jolted me from my sleep one morning while I was on a speaking trip to Denver. "Yes, of course. I'll stop on my way home."

Two days later, I got off the plane in San Francisco, rented a car, and drove five hours to Larry's central California home. His family was nursing him through the final agonizing stages of AIDS.

After a few hours talking and praying with Larry, I headed back up Interstate 5 to catch my plane to Hawaii. My heart ached for my friend and the suffering he was experiencing. As I sped along the dark and lonely stretch of the San Joaquin Valley highway, I kept thinking, "What a waste. What a waste of a life!"

Here was a young man, 32 years old, dying prematurely of a disease he contracted as a direct result of sin. What upset me was not so much the physical disease that was destroying Larry's immune system. I was angry at the spiritual disease that gave opportunity for the physical one to ravage his body. Somehow he had allowed sin to regain a foothold in his life, and its corruption delivered its full destructive force.

Larry was not some half-hearted Christian who warmed the back pew on Sundays while living for sin and self the other six days of the week. He had been a zealot, a man on fire for God. At one point in his life, he was leading worship at one of California's megachurches, singing and preaching the Gospel alongside me at outdoor rallies, and helping to recruit missionaries. He truly loved Jesus and wanted to serve Him and bring Him glory with his life.

Not all premature deaths among Christians are easily explained. This one was, and that made it all the more tragic. Larry had been hurt and disappointed by some Christians, and he allowed anger and bitterness to enter his spirit. He backslid for a season, got involved in a homosexual relationship that he knew was forbidden in the Bible, and as a result contracted AIDS.

Thirty hours before he died, I asked him what he'd say to young people if the Lord miraculously healed him and we went on the road for Jesus again. Without a moment's hesitation, he answered, "To the non-Christians, I would tell them there are no riches like the riches of Jesus. To the Christians, I would tell them that holiness is no option!"

Larry didn't make excuses or blame others for what happened to him. His bottom line was that he chose to disobey God's command to be holy (I Peter 1:16). Having confessed his sins and made his peace with God, I'm sure Larry is in Heaven today. But we can learn from his tragic fall. If we allow the beginnings of a spiritual disease to infect our soul, we could miss out on a good portion of our inheritance here on Earth.

Only God knows what Larry's life could have been had he been able to excise the spiritual cancer that had made the journey from thought to temptation to mental agreement to willful choice to action to death.

The subject of this chapter is the most serious and probably the most important in the book. The foundation for all other zeal— zeal for good works, spiritual gifts, evangelism, missions, etc., must be a zeal for God Himself and a desire to be like Him. That is the essence of holiness, to be like God. He is holy, so we must pursue His holiness. He is humble, so we must pursue His humility. He is righteous, so we must pursue His righteousness. To be like Him needs to be the all-consuming passion of our lives.

Tozer warned that a loss of awe for God's majesty and a low view of His divine Presence were the causes of a hundred lesser evils among us.[1] Every Christian should study the nature and character of God so we'll know who He is, and why we should strive to be like Him. Too often we focus on the preacher behind the pulpit or the singer on the stage as our models, and consequently, we seek God's hand rather than His face. The gift rather than the giver becomes the object of our worship. Count Zinzendorf, founder of the Moravian Missionary Movement once said, "I have one passion: it is Christ alone." Let that be our one desire too.

Getting Wholly Holy

> *"I pray God your whole spirit, and soul and body be preserved blameless unto the coming of our Lord Jesus Christ"* (1 Thess. 5:23 KJV).

Through the centuries of church history, the issue of holiness has generated hundreds of books and teachings. The many theoretical and practical books on the subject range from the helpful to the absurd to the impossible. Yes, some teach that holiness is an impossible ideal. They believe that we sin every day in thought, word or deed, and since nobody's perfect, why even try? On the other extreme are those who teach that once we obtain the "second blessing" or "crucify the old man," we attain a state of sinless perfection. This is unrealistic piety based on Scriptural double-talk. It leads to pride and ultimately to frustration. For obvious reasons, few people hold on to the doctrine of sinless perfection for very long.

---

1. A. W. Tozer, *Worship—The Missing Jewel of the Church.*

In the passage above, Paul prayed that the Thessalonian Christians would be "sanctified wholly." It must be possible then for Christians to live in a measure of victory and have a happy, holy zeal that covers our spirit, soul and body. Earlier Paul told these same Christians that it was God's will for them to be holy. He exhorted the Corinthians to cleanse themselves from "all filthiness of the flesh and spirit, perfecting holiness in the fear of God" (2 Cor. 7:1 KJV). Peter quoted the Old Testament command to be holy and told us that God has already provided all we need for us to obey that command. Hebrews 12:14 (NIV) says, "Without holiness, no one will see the Lord."

Facing Temptation

I was once discussing the subject of temptation with a Christian who looked me straight in the eye and said, "I don't have any problem with temptation, I just give in to it." His was obviously not the path to spiritual victory! Nevertheless, a proper understanding of temptation and how it works will help us in our pursuit of holiness.

First of all, we must see that *temptation is not sin*. Jesus was tempted "in all points like as we are, yet without sin" (Heb. 4:15 KJV). Temptation is the point at which a person decides whether or not to obey God's Word and receive His provision so he may keep from falling into sin. Temptation to do evil comes from the world, the flesh and the devil, whereas spiritual "testing" (sometimes called temptation) comes from God.

There are three main areas in which we are tempted. They are the lust of the flesh, the lust of the eyes and the pride of life (1 Jn. 2:16). In the wilderness Satan tempted Jesus in these three areas (Matt. 4:1-11; 27:40). His satanic majesty also showed up in the Garden of Eden with the same three temptations. In Genesis 3:6 he describes the tree as "good for food" (lust of the flesh), "pleasant to the eyes" (lust of the eyes) and "a tree desired to make one wise" (pride of life). You can be assured he hasn't changed his tactics. He will hit you in these three areas too.

Excuses, Excuses

The Lord supports with much patience and compassion those who honestly struggle with sin and genuinely want to be free of it. But He can't deliver us from sin if we keep making excuses for it. Tragically, our courts and prisons are loaded with people who blame an abusive parent, a bad neighborhood or a poor education for their evil doings. Psychologists support them by labeling sin a "sickness," and likewise, politicians are quick to blame societal pressures rather than moral failure. Perhaps the world will wake up and call sin SIN when the Christians do. We all need to take a hard look at ourselves from time to time to see if we're missing out on God's grace by excusing sins He longs to forgive. Sometimes we may not even recognize that we're excusing sin. To help spot these patterns, I have identified the following list of commonly used cop-outs for sin:

The "I'm Only Human" Excuse

This excuse blames Adam for all sinful actions. When a high standard of behavior is raised in the church, this person hoists the white flag of Original Sin as the reason for their evil deeds. Along with Paul they chime, "It wasn't me, but the sin that dwelleth in me!" Sin is made to seem like an implanted computer chip that dictates our actions. Aaron did some nifty blame-shifting when Moses confronted him about his lack of leadership in the golden calf situation: "I said unto them, Whosoever hath any gold, let them break it off. So they gave it me: then I cast it into the fire, and *there came out this calf*" (Ex. 32:24 KJV). The person with the "I'm only human" excuse rarely takes responsibility for his/her actions.

The "Wounded Spirit" Excuse

This is the favorite of people who use past hurts as an explanation for present sinful behavior. The worst examples of this are in court, where defense attorneys often call on pyschologists to excuse the most heinous of crimes because the perpetrator suffered from "repressed memories" or emotional stress.

This same "buck passing" mentality has entered the church as well. Confession of sin, restitution and brokenness at the foot of the

Cross are being replaced by endless digging into a person's past or subconscious to figure out why they do sinful or self-destructive things. I realize there are root causes for sin, but we still need to call it by its right name. We'll never conquer sin, until we stop excusing it, and bring it to the Cross.

The "Hereditary" Excuse

This excuse perceives sin as some type of genetic substance that is passed down through our bloodline. People are said to have an "Irish" or a "Latin" temper. Some cultures are actually proud of their reputation for certain sins. Some seem to major on lust, others on corruption, and still others on stinginess and greed.

Many of my ancestors were alcoholics. I have been told by some that should I ever "lose my religion," that's where I will end up. This is where I need to stand on my adoption into God's family. By faith I am a "new creation; the old has gone, the new has come" (2 Cor. 5:17 NIV). We are not in bondage to our ancestor's sins any more than we are in bondage to stealing because we have hands. The power released through the Cross and resurrection of Christ is real. Jesus came to save people from their sins (Matt. 1:21), even ones thought to be hereditary.

The "Blind God" Excuse

This one is usually only used by theologically sophisticated sinners. It goes something like this: "I am in Christ, clothed in His righteousness and justified, just as if I'd never sinned! Since I am clothed in the garments of Christ's righteousness, that's the way God sees me. When I sin, God the Father only sees me in Christ. All my sins—past, present and future—were taken care of at the Cross. Therefore, they are inconsequential."

Not only is this a theologically absurd view of imputed righteousness, but it makes the Lord of the Universe look like a bumbling old man who lets His children get away with murder. Of course, God sees when we sin. "The eyes of the Lord are in every place, beholding the evil and the good" (Prov. 15:3 KJV). Sin is more reprehensible in the life of a Christian than a non-Christian because he has the power to overcome and ought to know better. Concerning ministers who have fallen into sin, evangelist John Angell James said, "When a preacher of righteousness has stood in the way of sinners, he should never again open his lips in the congregation until his repentance is as notorious as his sin."[2]

The "Devil Made Me Do It" Excuse

I once heard a story about a man who saw Satan sitting on a curb crying. When he asked, "What's wrong?" the devil replied, "All those Christians are blaming me for things I never had a chance to do!"

This excuse is used by those who have run out of other excuses. When confronted about committing adultery, they say it was because they were possessed by a spirit of lust. When busted by the IRS for tax evasion, they say it was because of the spirit of greed. Others blame the territorial spirits who rule over cities and areas for influencing them toward evil.

The Bible teaches that Satan and his demons have much power, but it also teaches that the One who lives in you is greater than he who is in the world (1 John 4:4). The Christian has been given "all things that pertain to life and godliness" (2 Peter 1:3) and need not fear the enemy nor blame sinful actions on him. Satan may have influence over Christians to the extent that we give him access to areas of our lives. But he has no authority to control us. Even the man who was posessed by a "legion" of devils still had enough free will, *while he was still demonized,* to run to Jesus and worship Him (Mark 5:6). Let's give the devil his due, but not an inch more.

All of the above excuses have a grain of truth in them. We do have a bent towards sin in our nature, inherited from both Adam and our ancestors. We are affected by both our environment and the hurts we receive from others. We do have an enemy. And thankfully, we are clothed in Christ's righteousness. But we can never justify our sins before God by using any of these as excuses.

We are justified by faith in Christ alone, not by our good works or personal holiness. Nonetheless, our holy God has commanded

---

2. Charles Spurgeon, *Lectures to My Students.*

us to live holy lives and to do good works. And He has given us the means—through his own blood—to overcome sin and live victoriously.

Seven Steps to Overcoming Sin

1. Ask God for a true hatred of sin.

Holiness is sometimes described as "hating what God hates and loving what He loves." A pastor friend once counseled with an elderly sister in Christ about his struggle with lust. She listened patiently as he described his Dr. Jekyll and Mr. Hyde personality and this sin he said he abhorred. Then with motherly compassion and firmness, she said: "Your problem, honey, is you love your sin. That's why you can't stop. You don't really want to stop." He protested, "No, you don't understand, I hate it…" "No, my dear, you love it."

Finally, the truth set in. When my friend faced the truth with a ruthless honesty, he soon gained victory over the sin of lust. Only God can give us a true hatred for things that, because of our fallen state, we love to do. Be honest with God. He knows the truth anyway. You can say to Him, "I love the porno magazines or movies. I love to let my eyes wander at work or at church. I don't trust You to provide for my family if I don't cheat on my income tax…" Then pray, "Lord, help me to feel, even in my emotions, the way You feel about the things that sent You to the Cross."

2. Ask God for foresight on the pain that sin will cause Him, others and yourself.

If only Larry had taken the time to pray before he chose to engage in homosexual activity. If only he could have asked God, "If I go through with this, what could be the consequences?" He might have understood: I will break God's heart, nullify my Christian witness, hurt my family and my church, betray my friends, sin against this potential lover and maybe get AIDS.

If only some of the TV evangelists who were exposed for their sins would have taken time to seek God about the consequences of their actions. I believe the Lord would have shown them mental images of being publicly humiliated and weeping before the national media.

To those who are married and are playing mental games of adultery, my advice is simply: Stop doing it! If you're already in an affair, get out while there is still time! If you are single and are involved in immorality—get out of it! Get the help or counsel you need, or you will eventually pay for your sin with a great price.

3. Root out sinful thoughts.

All sin starts in the mind and in the heart, before working its way outward. James 1:14-15 (NKJV) says that "each one is tempted when he is drawn away by his own desires, and enticed. Then, when desire has conceived, it gives birth to sin: and sin, when it is full-grown, brings forth death." In other words, sin is the union of our free will with lust. First comes the seed of a thought into the mind. The thought takes root and becomes a temptation. When the will gives in to our lustful desire, then sin has "conceived" and sin starts growing like a strangling vine. While it's in our mind, there is still time to pluck it out before it causes any damage.

For example, let's examine that all-too-willing instrument of sin, our tongue. A slanderous thought about someone comes into your mind. You have a choice to make. Let the thought take root in your heart or reject it by choosing to believe the best about the person. Even if you allow the sin to take root in your mind, you can still stop it before it is "full-grown" and brings forth death. Of course, it is still a sin to think evil thoughts. But by stopping the mind from speaking out its evil thoughts, you prevent the sin from infecting others (through character assassination, bitterness, slander, etc.).

Hence, the need for bringing our thoughts into captive obedience to Christ (2 Cor. 10:5). At any time during sin's destructive journey from our thoughts, through our will, and into our actions, we can stop it.

4. Build walls around your spirit.

Solomon warned us that "he who hath no rule over his own spirit is like a city that is broken down, and without walls" (Prov. 25:28 KJV). It is crucial in pursuing holiness that we be pro-active in protecting ourselves against sin. Christian author Ray Stedman said, "Woe to the man who must learn his principles in the midst of a crisis." The adulterer often kicks himself after the fact over what he *could* have done to protect himself against sin's clutches. To be pro-active means to build walls ahead of time, *anticipating* that attacks will come.

For instance, a wall I have built in my life is to counsel a woman only with a third person present or to meet in public, not behind closed doors. The same is true when I need to ride in a car with another woman.

Once, when returning from a late night outreach, I noticed a woman whom I had seen at church walking alone up the street near our Youth With A Mission training center. Almost by instinct, I pulled over and asked if she wanted a ride. I gave her a 10-minute ride home and thought nothing of it. Soon I began receiving tapes and letters from the woman of a sexually implicit nature. I turned them over to other leaders to whom I am accountable, and they dealt with it by getting the woman psychiatric help. By God's grace, a third party, my son David, was in the car. Had he not been, she could have accused me of anything, and it would have been my word against hers. It was God's wake-up call to me to be careful.

First Lady Hillary Clinton once asked Billy Graham to have a meal with her. Billy politely declined saying, "I make it a policy never to have dinner alone with a beautiful woman." Billy was 73 at the time, but he let stand a "wall" that he had built 40 years before. That wall helped him maintain a blameless ministry.

The Lord knows better than you the areas in which you might be vulnerable. Ask Him to show you walls you can build around your spirit to protect yourself. He may well say something like, "Other people can go to that movie, but you can't. Others may be able to handle cable TV, but it's not healthy for you. Others may have liberty to drink alcohol, but it's not for you. Perhaps that platonic relationship with that woman is innocent and clean from her perspective, but for you, it's dangerous."

A few years ago, I began publishing books, tracts, audio and video tapes. Knowing the prevalent weakness among evangelists for greed, I set up an accounting procedure so that my income records from the sale of ministry materials was open to all local YWAM leadership. I also voluntarily refused any royalties or profits for the first four years of the publishing ministry.

Building these types of walls may seem rigid and even legalistic. But I've had to pick up the broken lives of people who didn't think they needed to build them. I'd much rather build walls and accept the "legalist" label gladly.

5. Be accountable to others.

One of the common characteristics of fallen brothers and sisters is the "Lone Ranger" syndrome. When I ask questions like "What church are you a member of? Or to whom are you accountable?" The answer is usually vague, like "I'm a member of the Body of Christ. I'm submitted to Jesus." Unfortunately, counseling clinics are full of Lone Rangers who have a "just me and Jesus" mentality. Somehow that isn't enough to keep them out of trouble.

Ask yourself the following questions: "Is there anyone in my life (besides Jesus) who can tell me 'no?' Am I close enough to anyone to be open and vulnerable with them? Is there anyone who knows my hurts, struggles and weaknesses enough to help by holding me accountable?"

Christian leaders, especially pastors, are often easy targets for the enemy because of their inability to answer these questions. A friend of mine who was a senior pastor once confessed to me that he had fallen into adultery—at a Bible conference no less! When I probed to find out how an otherwise godly father and husband could do this, he lamented that he had no close friend to help fix his troubled marriage. He was the pastor. He was supposed to have all the answers. Unfortunately, he didn't, and neither does anyone else. That is why we need accountability.

The "A" word (accountability) seems for some reason to scare people, but it should only scare you if you are a rebel. To voluntarily make yourself accountable to someone is an expression of humility. You are choosing *not* to think too highly of yourself (Rom. 12:3) and to heed Paul's warning in 1 Corinthians 10 about thinking ourselves too spiritually mature to fall. Proverbs 27:17 describes the relationship of friendship and accountability like this: "Iron sharpeneth iron; so a man sharpeneth the countenance of his friend." You recognize that to be as sharp as you can be for God you need another piece of iron to "rub" you and help you along your journey.

We are not merely a part of the "mystical body of Christ," but are fit together in relationships designed to nurture and assist one another much like a physical body. It's not just you and Jesus. It's you, Jesus and anybody else Jesus places you with in His overall plan. If you want to not just survive the long haul, but "finish the race (stoked) with joy" (Acts 20:24), then make the "A" word an "A" priority in your life.

6. Build yourself up in the Word.

These last two steps may seem so elementary that you'll be tempted to skip over them. Hang in there, dear reader, because if you are going to withstand the winds and rain of temptation your house will need to be built upon a rock. David warned us, "If the foundations be destroyed, what can the righteous do?" (Ps. 11:3 KJV). No one can exist very long without food. Eating good food helps keep our body strong and protects it from the diseases that would seek to destroy it. So it is also with spiritual food.

The Psalmist declared, "Thy word have I hid in mine heart, that I might not sin against thee" (Ps. 119:11 KJV). He knew that a steady diet of biblical food gave him an inner strength to help resist temptation and sin.

Jesus understood this well. When faced with the three temptations mentioned earlier, He responded by wielding the two-edged sword of God's Word in the devil's face. What is often overlooked, however, is that Jesus responded by quoting *memorized Scripture*.

Having the Word in your heart can keep you from yielding to temptation too. One such example for me was a time I got stranded at a Texas airport late one night. I managed to find the huge airport hotel, but in my jet-lagged, semi-comatose state, I couldn't find my room. Turning a corner, I literally walked into an attractive, partially inebriated woman. When I asked for directions, she said, "Follow me, I'll show you."

As we parted, she invited me to her room and shot me one of those "electrical vibe" looks. I turned away but later, as I sat in my room, staring at the wall through bleary eyes, I realized I was in the midst of a temptation.

"I wrote a book on how to witness for Christ in situations like that. Why didn't I witness to her?" I further reasoned, "I have a great marriage and family and I've never been unfaithful. Why should I start now?" Within a few minutes, I regained my presence of mind and prayed: "Lord, your Word says, 'No temptation has taken you but such as is common to man, but You are faithful and will not allow me to be tempted above my ability; but will with the temptation also make a way to escape, that you may be able to bear it' (1 Cor. 10:13). I come boldly to Your throne to find grace to help me."

I then called my wife, quoted another verse about the Lord giving His beloved sleep, and went to bed unscathed by the serpent of temptation. God's Word in my heart had helped me establish a link with reality and get His perspective on the situation. I didn't sin, even in my mind, but I was under attack. The shield of faith and the sword of the Spirit had given me the offensive and defensive weapons to withstand the enemy.

7. Recognize the "seasons" of temptation.

Another pro-active way to "get the jump on the devil" regarding temptation is to recognize that there are times or "seasons" when temptation is more likely to occur. This will help us to be ready. One of the comforting facts about temptation is that it's seldom constant. Peter tells us to "...greatly rejoice, though now *for a season*,...ye are in heaviness through manifold temptations..." (1 Peter 1:6 KJV). Jesus was tempted by Satan for a time and we are told that the devil "...departed from him *for a season*" (Luke 4:13 KJV).

The following are some "seasons" during which the wise servant of God would do well to keep his head down and eyes open because Satan's temptation is just around the corner:

After a great spiritual victory

Shortly after Elijah's powerful put-down of the prophets of Baal, Jezebel swore she would have him killed. The mighty prophet suddenly cowered in fear and asked God to save her the trouble by taking his life! (1 Kings 19:4). One minute he witnessed God's awesome power, the next he was suicidal. Likewise, Jeremiah proclaimed the glory and faithfulness of God to Pashur and exulted, "Sing unto the Lord, praise ye the Lord: for he hath delivered the soul of the poor from the hand of evildoers" (Jer. 20:13 KJV). Sounds good, so far, but look at the very next verse. "Cursed be the day wherein I was born: let not the day wherein my mother bare me be blessed."

Charles Spurgeon said, "The Lord seldom exposes his warriors to the perils of exaltation over victory; He knows how few of them can endure such a test, and therefore dashes their cup with bitterness."[3] Satan, as well as God, knows the tendency of the human heart to let down after a victory. While God allows the enemy to tempt us, we must be ready with the appropriate response.

Before any great achievement

When Joshua was about to lead the conquest of Canaan; when Jonah was about to bring a message of hope to Ninevah; and when Nehemiah was about to lead the rebuilding of Jerusalem's wall, all were tempted to quit. There will always be temptation to give up when getting ready to pioneer something new for the Lord. Satan has always been in the habit of destroying babies, whether they be physical or the newborn dreams and visions in the hearts of God's children.

Almost every victory I have ever achieved by faith has been preceded by a period of doubt and discouragement. Every David, before his Goliath is slain, will have his enemy curse and threaten him. So, be encouraged. Often the discouragement we feel is just a sign that good things are around the corner.

When we are in physical weakness

It is no accident that the devil hit Jesus with the temptation of His life while He was physically weak from a 40-day fast. Paul also was troubled by a "messenger of Satan" that he called a "thorn in the

---

3. Charles Spurgeon, *Lectures to My Students*.

flesh." Satan doesn't play fair. He loves to kick you while you're down physically. So beware when sickness strikes or you are physically weak. Satan wants us to give up or become ineffective in our Christian witness. But we can resist his attacks through prayer and Scripture. Have others pray with you—not just for healing, but that you'll be strong in spirit.

When troubles multiply

How would you like it if, in one day, you lost your family, your possessions, and your health? Then your wife slipped up beside you and said, "Curse God and die." That's what happened to Job. However, "Job sinned not, nor charged God foolishly" (Job 1:22 KJV) but maintained his integrity through it all. Like Job, we will be hit with temptation to doubt God when we experience a seemingly endless parade of trials and troubles. Be on the alert.

While this chapter has focused on how to recognize, withstand and overcome temptation, we must never forget that temptation itself is not the enemy. In fact, temptation can actually strengthen our character and thus help us in our goal of being like Jesus. Ask God to help you to see every trial, temptation and humiliation, every person who injures and vexes you as a means of grace to humble you and help you to be a partaker of His holiness (Heb. 12:10).

In all trials and temptations, "we are more than conquerors through him that loved us" (Rom. 8:37 KJV). So keep stoked on Jesus, our first love. All other fire in our lives must come out of the fire of His blazing holiness. God is an awesome God, but His awesomeness is not just because of His power, but because of His love and purity. Seek to make your life a reflection of His love and purity.

Stoker quote

"A lie will often travel the world before truth gets its boots on."

D.L. Moody

Chapter Six

Strange Fire

"And Nadab and Abihu, the sons of Aaron, took either of them his censer, and put fire therein and put incense thereon, and offered strange fire before the Lord, which he commanded them not."
Lev. 10:1 (KJV)

"My God, they're killing themselves in there." The FBI agent's chilling words stunned millions of TV viewers who watched in horror as the Branch Davidians' Waco, Texas, compound exploded in flames.

David Koresh and his embattled cult incinerated themselves rather than surrender to authorities on April 19, 1993. The 51-day siege began when cultists killed four federal agents who had come to arrest Koresh on weapons' charges. It ended with the deaths of 72 men, women and children in the Waco compound. Their ashes are a shocking reminder of what can happen when religious zeal runs amok.

The worst example in recent times is the Jonestown massacre of 1978. Who can ever forget the gut-wrenching news photos of 911 corpses found in that remote Guyana village? Rev. Jim Jones, who had coercively controlled his flock for years, persuaded them they were under attack and hundreds joined him in a final, poisoned cocktail. In 1994, another cult leader led dozens in a similar mass suicide at the Solar Temple in Switzerland.

Obviously, these three cases are extreme, but they illustrate how well-intentioned spiritual seekers can fall under the power of fanatical gurus, false prophets or church leaders. One of Satan's main strategies, if he cannot get us to backslide or cool off and become a pew-warmer, is to let our desire to serve God burn out of control. When that happens, both the voice of the Lord and common sense are lost in the raging flames of strange fire.

Through the centuries thousands of believers have been burned by "wolves in sheep's clothing" who use religion to justify their exploitations. Zealous people can be deluded into thinking that their zeal alone renders their actions acceptable with God. But Scripture shows that the Lord doesn't take kindly to His leaders, regardless of intentions, doing *His* work in *their* way.

A prime example is the incense offering of the priests Nadab and Abihu. The issue was not that they offered fire, but that it was a fire God had not commanded them to light. They did it on their own and suffered immediate consequences when God's own fire came upon them in judgment (Lev. 10:2).

God said He regretted making Saul king over Israel when His overzealous appointee decided to take the matter of the Amalekites into his own hands (1 Sam. 15:11). God then chose Samuel as His mouthpiece and declared a message that should still shake us today: "Behold, to obey is better than sacrifice, and to hearken than the fat of rams. For rebellion is as the sin of witchcraft, and stubbornness is as iniquity and idolatry" (1 Sam. 15:22-23 KJV). These verses need to be hung in big, bold letters on the refrigerator of every young zealot.

If not authorized by God, your zeal and fire are not only rebellion, but are the equivalent of witchcraft—no matter how seemingly spiritual they appear. It shows you are stubborn, lawless and idolatrous. Strange fire is nothing to play around with. You *will* get burned!

We don't have to look far to see "strange fires" burning all around us. The rise of religious fanaticism in the Middle East, Europe, North Africa and Asia have "burned" millions of people and shown a darker side of religions that proclaim peace while practicing war. In the United States, many non-Christians fear the rise of Christian political activism out of concern that it too will go awry and lead to theocracy.

The great English essayist, C.S. Lewis, once wrote, "I am a democrat because I believe that no man or group of men is good enough to be trusted with uncontrolled power over others. And the higher the pretensions of such power, the more dangerous I think it is both to the rulers and to the subjects.

"Hence, theocracy is the worst of all governments. If we must have a tyrant, a robber baron is far better than an inquisitor. The baron's cruelty may sometimes sleep, his cupidity at some point be sated; and since he dimly knows he is going wrong he may possibly repent. But the inquisitor, who mistakes his own cruelty and lust of power and fear for the voice of Heaven, will torment us infinitely because he torments us with the approval of his own conscience. His better impulses appear to him as temptations."[1]

Lewis is right. A fanatical leader who thinks God is telling him what to do is someone to be most feared.

Counterfeit Fire

In an age when we desperately need more integrity and spiritual reality, religious hypocrisy and hype are abounding. This counterfeit fire often masquerades as zeal, and even has some characteristics of the right stuff. But it is dark, deceptive and deadly.

While we don't always recognize the dangers of religious pride and legalism, the Bible certainly does. While many of its warnings relate to "sins of the flesh" such as sexual immorality, greed, selfishness, violence and deceit, Jesus directed his sharpest attacks at the more subtle sins of spiritual pride and phony self-righteousness.

---

1. Dave Hunt, *Whatever Happened to Heaven*, 23.

The New Testament books of Galatians, Colossians, Romans and Hebrews hit this fraudulent fire with the force of an oncoming train. For example, let's look at Paul's warning to the Romans about strange fire:

"Brothers, my heart's desire and prayer to God for the Israelites is that they may be saved. For I can testify about them that they are zealous for God, but their zeal is not based on knowledge. Since they did not know the righteousness that comes from God and sought to establish their own, they did not submit to God's righteousness" (Rom. 10:1-3 NIV).

In the above passage, we see three progressive, downward steps into the abyss of strange fire. First, they were ignorant of God's righteousness. As a result, they cooked up their own homemade brew of self-righteousness. The inevitable consequence of that choice is a blindness to true spirituality which is based on God's righteousness.

They had zeal, but "zeal not based on knowledge." What "knowledge"? The knowledge of God's righteousness. False fire is fueled by self-righteousness. It is self that starts the fire, self that keeps it going and self that gets all the credit for whatever results come from the egotistical blaze within.

As explained earlier, I was living a self-centered, hedonistic lifestyle devoid of any interest in God when Jesus saved me. It's abundantly clear to me that I didn't find Jesus; He found me! I lived in the joy of that salvation for a few years until strange fire began to burn in my soul.

I had begun to be disillusioned because of hypocrisy in the church. I saw Christian leaders living double lives and other Christians making moral compromises and becoming ensnared by materialism. The zeal that my mentors once modeled for me was now dismissed as youthful enthusiasm as they retreated into what I viewed as the devil's domain—lukewarm Christianity.

My response was to get increasingly tense and forceful. I lost the joy of the Lord. I lost my zeal for the lost and "holiness" became my consuming passion. I became extremely judgmental and critical of others who did not measure up to my standard.

My reasoning went something like this: I spent more time in prayer, Bible study and church attendance than others. Therefore, I was obviously more spiritual. I passed out more tracts, witnessed to more people (and believe me, I was counting) and gave a higher percentage of my income to God than others. Therefore, I was more committed and more pleasing to God.

I had become a 20th century Pharisee, a 24-carat fraud who had been deceived, not by the demons of lustful, loose living but by the "angel of light" types (2 Cor. 11:14) that freely assisted me in a zeal not based on proper knowledge. Concerned, loving brothers and sisters would approach me to try to help me out of my downward spiral, only to be met with a self-righteous response salted with Greek words, Scripture verses and statistics about the carnal state of the modern-day church.

By God's mercy and grace, He saved me out of the curse of legalism in the same sovereign way He saved my soul in the first place. He led me to a book called *The Calvary Road* by a British evangelist named Roy Hession whose testimony was eerily similar to mine. He too had measured spiritual success by a full calendar, big meetings and full altar-call responses. In his own words, "I was high and dry, dry because I was high."

He then met some Christians fresh from the East African revival who showed him that true spirituality was to walk down *The Calvary Road*. In just 100 pages, he taught what he had learned from those missionaries—that the Christian life is not a series of merit badges for the victories we win for God. True Christianity is a life of brokenness, humility and confessing and living as if God is all, and whatever we are and do is from and to Him.

Jesus saved His harshest rebukes, not for the prostitutes and publicans, but for the self-righteous Pharisees "who trusted in themselves that they were righteous" (Luke 18:9 NKJV). Paul's letter to the Galatians was like a laser-guided bomb aimed at the religious spirit of legalism prevalent in the church. You can almost feel the heat from his pen as he opened fire on the legalists with accusations of preaching a different gospel that was "perverted."

He pronounced a double "anathema"—the strongest form of curse and condemnation (Gal.1:6-9)—on those who added to the grace of Christ. He further declared such people "foolish" (the Greek word means "stupid") and said they had been "bewitched" (Gal. 3:1).

What happened to the Galatians can happen to us. We can begin, as I did, in the Spirit, and think we are perfected by the flesh (Gal. 3:3). After we have jumped in the salvation car, we ask Jesus to hop in the back seat and let us take over. We then live our Christian lives by a principle of law, rather than grace. We come up with rules, regulations and standards that are based on our view of the Bible, strongly influenced by our culture, denomination and even personality.

Legalism often leads to hypocrisy. The Christians who condemn others for going to movies will sometimes rent the same movies and watch them at home. Those who scorn those who smoke, quoting verses about our bodies being the temple of the Holy Spirit, sometimes indulge in the sin of gluttony and bombard their arteries with fat. And the list goes on…

You see, self-righteous, legalistic Christianity is always a dead-end street. You will ultimately incur condemnation because you will be judged by the same standards with which you judge others. (Matt. 7:1, Rom. 2:1). And make no mistake about it, when you become self-righteous, *you will* judge and criticize others and *you will* suffer the consequences.

This, I believe, is the main error of all non-Christian cults and religions. They, like the Pharisees, go about to establish their own righteousness and consequently cannot receive the righteousness of God. Our righteousness and relationship with God is either grace or no grace.

Zealous or Jealous

During my awful two-year sojourn in the wilderness of self-righteousness, I discovered another satanic fire extinguisher. At the same time I was passing judgment on those I deemed less spiritual, I was also jealous and envious toward those I deemed more spiritual or "successful" than I was. When another evangelist would have larger altar calls or another appeared more gifted, I would burn with envy. With other bad fruit came spiritual confusion and a muting of the Spirit's voice.

Eventually, I discovered truths that helped set me free. The first was a verse in the book of James that leapt off the page and into my understanding. "For wherever there is jealousy (envy) and contention (rivalry and selfish ambition) there will also be confusion (unrest, disharmony, rebellion) and all sorts of evil and vile practices" (Jas. 3:16, Amplified Bible).

That was it. The source of my confusion and unrest was jealousy. My envy produced a bitterness that ate away at my insides because I coveted what God had given to someone else. Once again, the root of this sin was self-righteousness.

The second discovery that blew my little Pharisical mind was that the same Greek word that is translated "zealous" is also translated "jealous."[2] While giving Moses the Ten Commandments, God described Himself as a jealous God (Ex. 20:5). And in Numbers 25:6-15, jealousy for God's honor is also spoken of in a positive way. (Remember Phineas?)

These contrast sharply with other Scriptures that show a dark and ungodly side of jealousy. Jealousy over someone else's success or giftings is simply another form of zeal gone bad. Whenever a spiritual leader becomes impressed with himself, real zeal takes a wrong exit off the highway of holiness and ends up in pride, confusion and ultimately deception. Study the roots of every major cult or aberrant Christian teaching and you'll find this is the common path to destruction. Every false religious leader, from Korah to Koresh, began with a zeal for truth, became deceived by self-righteousness, began judging others as inferior, became blinded by selfish ambition and jealousy, and started a strange fire that burned many in its path.

The following are four aspects of the strange fire of pride that might start with a flicker of self-righteousness and end up at a Waco or a Jonestown:

---

2. The Greek word *zelos* appears 17 times in the New Testament and its usage is split almost equally between positive zeal and negative envy or jealousy. See the *Complete Bible Library Greek-English Dictionary* (Vol. 2) 24.

Pride of Place

Symptoms include an exalted feeling of importance because of your position in the church, the family or the job. Zealous people sometimes are thrust into positions of leadership prematurely, without a sufficient test of their character. Their go-for-it attitude often cloaks a secret striving for power and backroom manipulation to keep it once they get it. The honor and exaltation of position goes to their head and causes them to forget the servant-leader model of Jesus.

Lucifer had this problem (Isa. 14:12-14), as did King Uzziah— "But after Uzziah became powerful, his pride led to his downfall" (2 Chron. 26:16 NIV). As British statesman Lord Acton once said, "Power corrupts, and absolute power corrupts absolutely." Often a simple title (Reverend, Director, Foreman, etc.) will go to someone's head so much that it clouds clear thinking and dulls the humility needed for true God-given exaltation (1 Pet. 5:6).

Once I counseled a blame-shifting, jealous, striving young man who thought he should have been made an elder in a local church. He claimed he was overlooked for the position because of the church leaders' "insecurity." It was "obvious" (only to him) that his giftings would overshadow them, and they feared being in the presence of such greatness.

I showed him a couple of verses from the Psalms. "For promotion cometh neither from the east, nor from the west, nor from the south. But God is the judge: he putteth down one, and setteth up another" (Ps. 75:6-7 KJV). I said "Bro, you can accuse all those guys of anything you choose if it will make you feel better, but the fact is, you're not in leadership in this church because *God* didn't put you there. So if you are wondering how such a gem as yourself was passed over you'd better go to God and find out why *He* didn't release you into that position."

Pride will cause us to strive after position, and pride will cause us to think more highly of ourselves than we ought when we are in a position. The next time you feel you are in a place of authority and responsibility because you're so special remember the words of Francis of Assisi when Brother Masseo, one of his subordinates asked him why God chose him for leadership…"His most holy eyes have not found among sinners any smaller man, nor any more insufficient and sinful, therefore He has chosen me to accomplish the marvelous work which God has undertaken; He chose me because He could find none more worthless, and He wished to confound the nobility, the strengths, the beauty and the learning of this world."[3]

Pride of Race

A few years ago, I was awaiting takeoff in a Garuda Airlines plane at Jakarta International Airport in Indonesia. When the pilot gave the usual greetings and safety instructions, his English was so good I was sure he was an American. I settled back into my seat, closed my eyes, and rested with the confidence that we were headed for a safe flight.

At that moment the still, small voice of the Holy Spirit seemed to whisper into my ear. "Danny, why does it make you feel more secure to know that an American is flying this plane?" My eyes popped open as I began to ponder the implications of the question. As I gazed blankly at the air-sickness bag, the answer came loud and clear. "Because I think Americans are more intelligent than Indonesians and therefore would make better pilots!" I was astonished at what God was revealing to my starred and striped mind. I was prejudiced. I was proud of my American culture to the putting down of others. I was guilty of the *pride of race*.

Racial or cultural pride can lead to racism, and racism can lead to many other evils. Most of us would never come right out and say that because we are white, black, American, German, Baptist or Charismatic we are better than someone else. But deep within us, many have that root of racial or cultural pride. Sadly, many who call themselves Christians have even used the Bible to try to justify their racist beliefs and practices.

Humanity must be prone to this type of pride or the Bible wouldn't devote so much attention to it. Jewish racial pride blinded them to the Gospel. The Romans, who also had a problem with

---

3. J. O. Sanders, *Spiritual Leadership* (Chicago: Moody Press) 40.

racism, had to be reminded to "receive one another...to the glory of God" (Rom. 15:7 NKJV). Peter had to be broadsided by the Holy Spirit with a rooftop vision to be reminded that God had "cleansed" the Gentiles. Years later, Paul rebuked him over the same issue (Acts 10:9-16, Gal. 2:11-16). The New Testament makes it perfectly clear that "in Christ Jesus" no race, gender or social status is superior to another, but that we are "*equal*" (Gal. 3:28, Col. 3:11).

Pride of Face

Each of our four types of pride get progressively worse, like the downward steps into a dungeon. Pride of face is a superiority based on your physical appearance. It is exemplified in a statement "Broadway Joe" Namath made in the brashness of his youth when he began to play in the National Football League: "I can't wait until tomorrow, because I get better-looking every day!"

We might not come across that arrogantly, but often we are guilty of the same preoccupation with physical beauty. How much time do we spend getting our body ready to go to church and how much time do we spend getting our spirit ready? How much of our desire to get in shape or be "buff" comes from a desire to impress others with our outward appearance? The cosmetic industry reaps billions of dollars from a culture that despises physical deformity and idolizes youth and beauty. If you have the money, you can get your body painted, plucked, tucked, stretched or pinned. As Christians we must recognize the spirit of the age lest it seduce us into the same narcissistic mentality.

Both Paul and Peter warned women not to be overly concerned with physical appearance but to "clothe themselves in godliness, humility and good works" (1 Tim. 2:9-10, 1 Peter 3:3-4). Solomon declared in his famous description of the virtuous woman, "Charm is deceitful and beauty is passing, But a woman who fears the Lord, she shall be praised" (Prov. 31:30 NKJV).

Men are likewise prone to overindulge in mirror-watching and body work. Millions of us get our hair styled (or replaced), adorn ourselves with earrings, chains and other jewelry, or pump iron to get that ultimate buff appearance. During my teens and early twenties, I worked on a golden, surfer tan. Now I'm paying the price for that overexposure to sun. Not long ago, I had a skin cancer removed from my chest, and the 1 1/2 inch scar will be a reminder to me that dark suntans and all other outward beauty eventually fade away. Pride of face leads away from the true, godly attractiveness of the heart.

Pride of Grace

By far the most hideous form of pride, which is certain to quench real zeal, is spiritual pride. I use that term loosely, as it is actually a contradiction of terms. Technically, if you are truly spiritual you won't be proud, and if you're proud it proves you are not spiritual.

Spiritual pride is often deceptive because of its religious nature. "The pride of your heart has deceived you" (Obadiah 3 NIV). Some of us don't realize that our love of human praise, our intense need to be noticed, our drawing attention to ourselves in conversation, or our "puffed up" feelings about our successes or giftings are evidences of spiritual pride. Sure, we can justify them by declaring our need for affirmation, but God is the only one who can give us the affirmation we really need.

Prideful leaders often want to be treated as something special, and when they are not, they can pass off their anger and impatience as "righteous indignation" over disrespect for authority. Carnal preoccupation with the opinions of others is a trap that brings us into bondage. Testimonies loaded with the personal pronoun "I" should make us suspicious immediately. Spiritual pride is likely to be lurking behind a godly veneer.

The pride of grace is particularly reprehensible because it's a pride over gifts and abilities freely given to us by God. Paul challenged the Corinthians with the following question, "What do you have that you did not receive? And if you did receive it, why do you boast as though you did not?" (1 Cor. 4:7 NIV).

How can we be proud of something which was none of our doing in the first place? It is because we begin in the Spirit and end up in the flesh (Gal. 3:3). We begin broken, lost and desperate at the foot of the cross; "Just as I am without one plea." As we grow in grace and God begins to use us, we slowly become impressed more with the gift and the vessel containing the gift (ourselves) than with the Giver. Pride then enters with all its ugly consequences, and strange fire begins to burn.

How else do we explain lowly, poor-as-a-church-mouse country preachers who become successful and then strut like a peacock when "on stage"? How do we fathom a former alcoholic or heroin addict who, because of spiritual success, becomes aloof, untouchable and unaccountable? It is because they've become proud of abilities God has given them. When this happens, you can be sure they are in for a fall—as sure as sparks fly upward (Prov. 16:18).

One of the saddest stories in the Bible is about a man who was terminally ill with spiritual pride. King Uzziah was a God-fearing monarch who was successful in both war and peace. The Scripture declares he was "greatly helped until he became powerful. But after Uzziah became powerful, his pride led to his downfall" (2 Chron. 26:15-16). He then decided to offer incense in the temple, an act that was expressly forbidden to anyone but the priests. Eighty priests tried to talk him out of it, but he went ahead anyway. Why? Because he was the king, and he could do anything he jolly well pleased. His arrogance was short-lived. As he burned incense, God judged him and struck him with leprosy.

His epitaph reads, "And Uzziah the king was a leper unto the day of his death, and dwelt in a several [separated] house, being a leper; for he was cut off from the house of the Lord" (2 Chron. 26:21 KJV).

Spiritual pride is a stench in the nostrils of a holy God who humbled himself to become a man and then humbled himself even further to go to the cross (Phil. 2:5-11). Spiritual pride is inexcusable in the life of a Christian because of the nature of free grace and the reproach that such pride brings on the gospel.

To put it crudely, pride stinks! It stinks because it is the antithesis of who God is and how he governs His Kingdom. It stinks because the very expression of God's humility—Jesus Christ—is misrepresented by professing Christians who exemplify satanic principles of self-love, self-promotion and self-exaltation.

I'd like to close this section with a warning from a South African prophetic teacher named Andrew Murray.

"It is from our pride above everything else that we need to be delivered. Accept every humiliation, look upon every fellowman who tries and vexes you as a means of grace to humble you. Use every opportunity of humbling yourself before your fellowman as a help to remain humble before God...If you could see what every stirring of pride does to your soul, you would beg of everyone you meet to tear the viper from you, though with the loss of a hand or an eye."[4]

4.   Andrew Murray, *Humility* (Whitaker House) 76, 98.

Stoker quote

"I have one passion; it is Christ."
Ludwig Von Zinzendorf

Chapter Seven

Stoke Chokers

*"For I can testify about them that they are zealous for God,
but their zeal is not based on knowledge."*
Romans 10:2 (NIV)

On an overcast Saturday afternoon I was leading a group of zealous new converts out to the Santa Cruz Garden Mall for an afternoon of street witnessing. After one encounter, I noticed out of the corner of my eye that one of my "pupils" was engaged in an intense dialogue with some bearded young men with Bibles under their arms. It didn't take long to figure out that they were from the infamous "Children of God" cult. While many followers professed a sincere faith, the COGs' leadership had become increasingly authoritarian, exploitive and unbiblical in their practices. The COGs were notorious for ripping off new converts from the Jesus Movement revival. And these guys were bearing down on young Jim like a heat-seeking missile.

I quickly got my "gospel gun" ready and walked over to do battle with these unsuspecting knaves. How dare they go after one of my "little ones"! To my shock, I found myself outgunned and totally unprepared for this rescue mission. Although I was just a year old in my faith, I thought that with my knowledge of the Bible I could take on any cultist. But these guys were not only able to quote reams of King James Version Scripture, they were, at least outwardly, more committed and zealous than anyone I had ever met.

Within 10 minutes, I was on the defensive without much defense. I'm sure my eyes resembled a racoon facing truck headlights! Every question I asked was answered with a Bible verse. "Don't you work at a job?" I asked one of them. "Labor not for the food that perisheth," he responded. "Where do you get your food?" "Take no thought for your life, what you shall eat or what you shall drink," came the reply. "Where do you live?" "Foxes have holes, birds have nests, but the Son of Man hath no where to lay his head." "What about bank accounts and savings?" "Lay not up for yourselves treasures on earth."

They challenged me to join them. When I asked them what they did all day long they simply explained that they worshipped, prayed, read the Bible (and the Bible only) and told people about Jesus. Within an hour, I was seriously considering obeying their exhortation to "forsake all" and follow them. Meanwhile, my young disciples were freaking out that their leader was being persuaded to join a group that they already perceived as being weird.

By some wise counsel, some fasting and prayer and the grace of God, I didn't join the COGs. However, I did learn an important lesson: Zealous people can be deceived and are sometimes even more prone to fall for the seductive temptations of the devil, especially when dressed in religious clothing.

The following "stoke-chokers" are some diseases that I've encountered in my journey to real zeal. Look behind the humor to see the dangers of these diseases. If left to grow unchecked, they can be fatal in the life of the believer.

Areopagitus—Fad Fascination (Acts 17:19-31)

One of Paul's preaching venues included an interesting place in Athens called the Areopagus. It was a place where both the locals and the visitors would gather to discuss the latest religious and philosophical ideas being bandied about in Greek culture. The main qualification for the content of their conversation was not its truth or its value, but simply that it was "new." They were the first century equivalent of the investigative reporter who wanted to be the first to break the latest news to the public.

I have met many Christians infected with "Areopagitus"—the disease of chasing spiritual fads. In the mind of the Areopagite, the "new" revelation or light on "present truth" will be the key to turning the tide for world revival. Zealous people seem more prone than most to chase the proverbial rabbit in hopes that, when they catch it, they will find the answer.

Soon after I became a Christian, I came in contact with "deliverance" ministries. They thought demons were everywhere. Gluttony demons were in the refrigerator and speed demons under the hood of the car. Getting your personal demons cast out was the answer to all of life's ills. Then there was the "shepherding" movement. If everyone would just be committed, submitted and fitted under one of God's under-shepherds, then the church would be true to the elusive New Testament pattern and the Kingdom would surely come.

In the 1980s, a U.S. President's sister introduced us to "inner healing." And in the mid-90s, the crucial biblical concept of resisting the devil began to be over-shadowed by a fad of spiritual warfare that, in some instances, sheds more light on Satan than God.

Unfortunately, some zealous people resemble butterflies that flit from one spiritual trip to another. All of the above emphases are good and needed, but only when in balance with the rest of Scripture. Jesus said, "Every scribe which is instructed unto the kingdom of heaven is like unto a man that is an householder, which bringeth forth out of his treasure things *new* and *old*" (Matt. 13:52 KJV). God does emphasize various truths at different times in history, but be sure your fascination is with what God is speaking to you, not what's on the Christian "news"!

Nicolaitan's Disease—The Clergy-Laity Trap (Rev. 2:6)

Jesus declared to the church of Ephesus that He hated the teaching of the Nicolaitans. This was an over-emphasis on a spiritual hierarchy that exalted the clergy over the laity or the regular people in the church. This later developed into the church pyramid structure that ascended from elders to priests to bishops to archbishops and other high authorities.

One sure-fire way to pour water on your stoke for Jesus is to put too much responsibility for your life and actions into the hands of a spiritual leader. One of the great truths that Luther and the Reformers laid their lives down for, was that all believers are priests and therefore ministers of God (1 Peter 2:5,9).

Jesus said His sheep would know His voice. We are individually responsible to obey it. While there is safety in counsel (Prov. 11:14), we must be sure we're not fulfilling someone else's plan for our lives. Unfortunately, in some churches and ministries there are still domineering men and women who love to control the destinies of others. Make sure that Jesus is the one controlling your destiny.

Anthrophobia—The Fear of Man (Prov. 29:25)

In 1881 when the British ruled India, a group of Salvation Army workers decided to "open fire" on Bombay and preach the gospel of Christ. Fearing Hindu and Muslim riots, Deputy Commissioner John Godfrey Smith stopped an open-air praise march led by Frederick Tucker: "In the name of Her Majesty, Queen of England and Queen Empress of India, I order you to disperse." Tucker then raised his hand to silence the crowd. His voice rang out clear and fearless: "In the name of His Majesty, the King of Kings and Lord of Lords, I command *you* to step aside."[1]

His boldness cost him a month in jail, but soon Tucker won a court battle that stopped official persecution of Salvationists. And he soon pioneered ministries in Calcutta, Madras, Pune, Lahore and Colombo. Tucker had learned a lesson as ancient as the wisdom of Solomon: "The wicked flee when no man pursueth: but the righteous are bold as a lion" (Prov. 28:1 KJV). The fear of man has doused the fire of many a would-be zealot.

---

1. Richard Collier, *The General Next to God* (Fantana) 81.

Getting free from this bondage to the opinions of others is an essential requirement for a truly stoked believer. Paul told the Corinthians it was "a very small thing" what they or anyone else thought. It was the Lord's opinion he was most concerned about (1 Cor. 4:1-5). Well-meaning friends can criticize us right out of fulfilling our destiny in God.

C.T. Studd, the all-star British cricket player turned pioneer missionary to Africa told an insightful story about the critical eyes of our fellowman: "Remember the miller's donkey? The miller, son and donkey went to market. The miller rode the donkey and people exclaimed, 'Cruel man, riding himself and making his son walk.' So he got down and his son rode. Then people slanged, 'What a lazy son for riding while his poor old father walks.' Then both father and son rode, and the people said 'Cruelty to animals, poor donkey.' So they got down and carried the donkey on a pole, but folks said, 'Here are two asses carrying another ass.' Then all three walked and people said, 'What fools to have a donkey and not ride it.' So let's go ahead with our work for God and care not about what folks say. Had I cared for the opinions of others, I would never have been a missionary."[2]

Hardening Of The Arteries—Traditionalism (Matt. 15:7-9)

Someone has said, "A rut is a grave with both ends kicked out." In other words, to get stuck in a rut is the equivalent of death even though you're still alive. Jesus warned the Pharisees that they were nullifying the commandments of God by their tradition. As a result, they were "teaching for doctrines the commandments of men" (Matt. 15:9).

Most revivals start with a man with a message that becomes a movement, that ends up a mausoleum. This is because by nature we love to categorize how, and by what means, God will pour out His Spirit. History shows that every two or three generations God needs to raise up a fresh voice who has the courage to break free from the

---

2. *World Shapers* (Shaw Publishing) 12.

traditions of men to do things differently as God leads him. Such men and women recognize that the tradition was good for its time, but now, having served its purpose, the old wineskin is disregarded in favor of the new (Matt. 9:17).

In the past three decades, visionary leaders have changed the traditions, but not the message of various churches and missions.

Back in the early 1970s, Chuck Smith was a pastor who felt some of his denomination's traditions were putting him in a rut and quenching God's Spirit. He launched out on his own, welcomed the unchurched, changed the worship style, and emphasized simple verse-by-verse Bible teaching. Years before, God had given Chuck's wife, Kay, a vision for the aimless hippie generation and she prayed out her heart for them. Soon hippies came pouring into Calvary Chapel, receiving Christ and forming a church movement that has impacted the world. Today Calvary Chapel regularly has over 20,000 in attendance. It has spawned over 700 churches and launched a worldwide teaching and music tape ministry.

Bill Hybels was a young Bible college student when an older man challenged him about the traditional form of a Sunday morning worship service. The older man wondered what would happen if Sunday mornings were more evangelistic and directed more to reach the unchurched. Bill tried it and now his Willow Creek Community is one of the largest churches in America. Many others have followed his "user-friendly" model, using the church service itself as an evangelistic tool.

In 1960, Loren Cunningham and George Verwer were young men who felt the traditional approach to missions was missing out on a vast resource pool of potential missionary candidates—young people. Separately, they both formed a "new wineskin" that served as a vehicle to recruit youth into missions. Youth With A Mission and Operation Mobilization were born and continue to mobilize young people from every continent to get stoked on missions.

Koinonitus—Overdose of Christian Fellowship

The Greek word *koinoneia* is translated in the New Testament as fellowship or communion. We are commanded to share our life together (Heb. 10:25), and we see fellowship modeled in the Gospels and Acts (Acts 2:42). However, even a good practice like fellowship can develop into a "country club" mentality that takes a "holier than thou" attitude toward sinners.

A neglect of consistent outreach to the world and a healthy rubbing of shoulders with non-Christians will surely kill our zeal for God. In the name of holiness, we separate ourselves from the very people we are called to reach. We arrange our schedules around our church meetings. We try to work on jobs with Christians lest we should be defiled by the world. When we socialize, we go to Christian potlucks and seek to build relationships with fellow believers. When we play tennis, we play with Christians. When we play baseball, we do it in a Christian league with Christian coaches, players and umpires on a field that has an Icthus fish on the scoreboard!

We are not called to be isolated from the world, but insulated *in* the world. Jesus said, "I have not come to call the righteous, but sinners to repentance" (Luke 5:32 RSV). After talking to hundreds of young Christians over many years, I've concluded that the average Christian has very few, if any, meaningful relationships with non-Christians after about two years since his or her conversion. The tragedy is that often we are *taught* to shun the world in the name of not being conformed to it or in love with it (Rom. 12:1).

Let's not forget that "God so loved the world..." (John 3:16). And when we speak of holiness, we must keep in mind that the primary purpose of being filled with the *Holy* Spirit is that we might be witnesses for the Lord. Jesus, who was the holiest person who ever lived, was called a "friend of sinners" (Matt. 11:19). A good portion of his social life was spent with prostitutes, publicans and sinners.

Where did we get the idea that to sit around and scratch each others' backs in some sort of spiritual mutual admiration society was the way to true holiness? Perhaps it would serve us well to compare our modern forms of separatist piety to the true "Jesus style" holiness that attracted people to the Savior.

The great German churchman Dietrich Bonhoeffer once said "The church is not the church unless it exists for the sake of others."[3]

3. Dietrich Bonhoeffer, *The Cost of Discipleship* (New York: Macmillan).

Some would disagree and contend that the church exists for the Lord. Of course, it is true that we are to love God with all our heart, mind, soul and strength. But Jesus gave us three other directives—to love our neighbor as ourselves, to love one another (our family in Christ) and to proclaim His good news to every creature. These three all involve an outward focus that springs forth from an inward devotion to God.

We need each other, living stones built together to be God's temple, and the mortar that bonds us together is "the love of God, and the fellowship of the Holy Spirit" (2 Cor. 13:14 NIV). We must keep in mind, however, that we are to be a city on a hill, a light in the darkness to give Christ's light to a dark world. Consider this challenge from a contemporary writer:

"I simply argue that the cross again be raised at the center of the marketplace as well as on the steeple of a church. I am recovering the claim that Jesus was not crucified in a cathedral between two candles, but between two thieves: on the town garbage heap, at a crossroads so cosmopolitan that they had to write his title in Hebrew, Latin and Greek, at the kind of place where cynics talk smut, thieves curse and soldiers gamble. Because that is where he died and that is what he died about and that is where the church should be and what churchman ought to be about."

Spiritual Myopia—Tunnel Vision (Prov. 29:18)

Proverbs 29:18 (KJV) says, "Where there is no vision, the people perish." One sure way to quench your stoke is to develop a myopic, introspective, self-centered viewpoint on life. Spiritual tunnel vision doesn't allow you to see into the future or much beyond yourself and your needs. This type of myopia can't sustain any fire for God because there is nothing there to burn. Myopia is a self-centered wasteland.

One of the chief causes of spiritual myopia (lack of vision) is a bad memory. Peter opened his second epistle by urging his readers to "...give all diligence" to adding seven qualities to their faith. He then warned that he who lacked these qualities is "blind, and cannot see afar off, and hath forgotten that he was purged from his old sins" (2 Pet. 1:9 KJV). Apparently such memory loss shrinks our vision so we "cannot see afar off."

The apostles may have also struggled with this problem. They had received a clear command from Jesus to "make disciples of all nations," but they didn't break any speed records in taking the Gospel out of Jerusalem. It wasn't until the Antioch church commissioned Paul and Barnabus—neither of whom were part of the original 12 apostles—that a visionary effort was made to reach out beyond Palestine. Don Richardson, a respected missionary and author, theorizes that the apostles' reluctance to obey the Great Commission is the "hidden message of Acts."[4]

The view that Jerusalem was the center of the Earth, however, was not exclusive to the First Century Jewish Christians. In my travels in the United States, I often encounter well-meaning believers who have no focus beyond their local church or community. Statistics released by the U.S. Center for World Missions show that the vast majority of church resources, people and money are used by the churches themselves.[5]

One of the best ways to cure spiritual myopia is to begin regular times of intercessory prayer for the nations. Once you start praying for a particular nation or people group, God begins to open your eyes to those fields that are ready for harvest.

Of course, many Christians prefer to keep the focus on themselves. After one of our intercession times, a young student questioned my love for our staff and students because we were praying more for Asia than for their individual needs.

"I'm sorry you don't think I love and pray enough for the people here. I do love them," I replied. "But let me tell you who else I love. I love one billion Muslims who bow down five times a day in obedience to a law that can never save them. I love 800 million Hindus whose millions of gods keep them in bondage to fear and

---

4. Don Richardson, *Eternity in Their Hearts* (Regal Books) 156.
5. Statistically, the survey divides the world into three categories: the reached, the reached but resistant, and the unreached. The "reached" nations receive some 87.2 percent of all missions finances, 99 percent of all Gospel TV and radio broadcasts, and 90.9 percent of all missionaries. Only a tiny fraction go to unreached peoples.

poverty. I love 300 million Buddhists who travel an eight-fold path to nowhere. I love 200 million tribal peoples who worship animal and demon spirits, and I love countless others who are on the same pathway to hell. That's who I love!"

The reason that people are perishing without Jesus is because we lack vision for the world. Jesus told us to lift up our eyes and look on the harvest fields. He didn't ask us to look into a mirror of introspection and self-centeredness.

In his "prayer encyclopedia," *Operation World*, author Patrick Johnstone calls this generation "the largest ingathering of people into the Kingdom of God that the world has ever seen."[6] The church of Jesus Christ now numbers approximately 500 million born-again believers, and it's growing rapidly. The reason is that men and women of vision are praying for the unreached masses and taking the Gospel to them.

D.U.D.S.–Deficient Understanding of Divine Sovereignty

"Sit down young man. You are an enthusiast. When God pleases to convert the heathen, He'll do it without consulting you or me!"[7] So spoke the Baptist deacon as a rebuke to William Carey who presented the spiritual needs of India at a prayer meeting near London.

The 21-year-old Carey sat down in his body, but remained standing in his heart and went on to publish a booklet that would rock the Western world out of its apathy toward missions. He then sailed for India, where he established churches, translated the Bible, started a Bible College and helped abolish unjust Indian laws. Had he "sat down," he would have been inoculated against real zeal by giving in to the "D.U.D.S." virus—a passive, lazy viewpoint on man's responsibility cloaked in the language of God's sovereignty.

The subject of Divine Sovereignty and how it is reconciled with man's free will has been debated for years and my intention here is

---

6. Patrick Johnstone, comp., *Operation World* (Zondervan) 24-25.
7. J. Herbert Kane, *A Concise History of Christian Missions* (Baker) 85.

not to exhaust the arguments. When asked about the subject, evangelist Charles Spurgeon said, "I don't try to reconcile friends." Nonetheless, I believe something should be said on the subject lest we wait in vain for God to do something He's told *us* to do.

Once I was struggling with the theological implications of the conflicting biblical doctrines of Calvinism, which emphasizes predestination, and Arminianism, which emphasizes man's free will, when I felt the voice of the Spirit say: "I'm God, you let me take care of My Sovereignty. You take care of your responsibility." In an instant, I felt like I was set free. I stopped trying to figure it out and concentrated on the work God has given me to do.

I have seen missionaries give up, churches split and friendships broken because of D.U.D.S. Some Calvinists think an emphasis on free will robs God of His sovereignty, while the other side, the Arminians, think that too much emphasis on sovereignty is a cop-out. My point is, it doesn't matter. Yes, the Bible speaks of God's foreknowledge, election and predestination. No matter how you interpret those passages, they do not negate the other explicit commands to obey what God has told us to do.

The D.U.D.S.-infected deacon in William Carey's church had allowed a misunderstanding of divine sovereignty to blind him to the clear command of Jesus to reach all the nations with the Gospel. Isn't it ironic that, for some people, the more they study the Bible, the less they obey the Bible?

Because of my finite mind, I must throw my feeble hands up and say, "I don't understand it all, but I trust You." The Bible says God wants us to know Him, but that doesn't mean we can understand everything about an infinite personal God. I want my own children to know and understand me too, but I don't mind if they can't figure out the intricacies of my muscular, neurological or skeletal systems. It's more important that they know my character and trust me.

The bottom line is that we are obligated to obey the Lord. The way we prove to be His disciples is to "continue in His Word" (John 8:31), and the way we make disciples is to teach them to obey all Jesus commanded us (Matt. 28:19-20). Jesus said, "Blessed are they that hear the word of God, and keep it" (Luke 11:28 KJV).

William Booth, toward the end of his life, warned of five dangers that would plague the church of the 20th century:

Religion	without	the Holy Spirit
Salvation	without	Lordship
Forgiveness	without	Repentance
Heaven	without	Hell
Christianity	without	Christ

All of these heresies will flourish in the church if we don't develop a balanced perspective of God's soveriegnty, His character and His commands.

Spiritual Arthritis—Problems in the Joints

When I first became a Christian, I enjoyed a short-lived honeymoon of optimism with regards to how believers related to each other. Not having been raised in an evangelical church, I presumed the fellowship of the saints was full of love, good deeds, forgiveness and servanthood. I was in for a rude awakening. I soon discovered that the church was far from being one big happy family. The people of God seemed to have the same anger, resentments, bitterness and hatred for each other that I had seen in the world. As I continued to read the New Testament, I discovered that sins like hatred, envy, bitterness, adultery, Christians suing each other, extortion and even murder were spoken of frequently as problems among Christians. These, and other "social" sins plagued the first century church just like they do today. I also discovered six of the Ten Commandments had to do with sinning against each other, as well as God. It bugged me, being a young evangelist, that the New Testament didn't speak more about witnessing and reaching the lost. God seems to be saying, "First things first. How do you relate to one another?"

I also discovered another interesting fact about Christian relationships. Our unity and love for each other has a direct evangelistic impact on the world. Jesus said the world would know we were His disciples by our love for each other (John 13:35), and our unity would demonstrate that the Father sent the Son into the world (John 17:21-23).

Paul taught that a godly husband/wife relationship would be a visual aid for the world to see Christ's love for the church (Eph. 5:22-23). A practical demonstration of love for neglected widows in the early church led to "the number of disciples in Jerusalem multiplying greatly" (Acts 6:1-7). In the Psalms, we are promised a blessing of "life forevermore" if we dwell together in unity (Ps. 133). This apparently refers to non-Christians receiving a blessing from our love for each other.

Recent missions surveys show that over 80 percent of all missionary candidates do not last on the field past their first term (four years). Can you guess why? No, it's not sickness, disease, lack of support, persecution, visa problems or even the devil. Surveys on returning missionaries show conclusively that most quit because they can't get along with the other believers. Jealousy, greed, power struggles, pride and a host of other selfishly oriented maladies are the main affliction in the missionary community.

Spiritual arthritis refers to this problem. I have witnessed personally to hundreds of people who have told me the main stumbling block to them becoming a Christian is that Christians don't act like Christ. For us in the Body of Christ, it's not how we relate to the head that's the issue, but how we relate to the other members of the Body that are adjacent to us—in the joints.

A few years ago I was in a serious relationship conflict with another Christian leader. It was not only killing my joy and choking my stoke, but there were other consequences. Although I never would have admitted it then, I can honestly say I hated the person. When we met together to resolve the conflict we began to pray. In prayer, I had a vision of the blockage in the spiritual realm of God's blessing on our evangelistic work. I began to weep and weep. Deep repentance came into my spirit. Self-justification, self-righteous anger, hatred and revenge left as I had a revelation of what our conflict was doing to the heart of God.

A fellow-minister said to me once, "I love the ministry. It's the people that I can't stand!" This was said in jest, but there's more truth in that statement than many of us would like to admit. If you feel like you "can't stand" people, you had better get your feelings adjusted to the facts because the ministry *is* people. Here is a prescription for some relief to the red, sore, swelling in the spiritual joints in the Body.

1) Realize conflicts will come. Starry-eyed optimism is unrealistic. We live in an imperfect world.
2) Try to put yourself in the shoes of the person you're having conflict with (Gal. 6:1).
3) Don't try to resolve conflict in the heat of your spirit. You may say and do things you'll later regret. "A soft answer turneth away wrath" (Prov. 15:1 KJV). "The anger of man does not achieve the righteousness of God" (Jas. 1:20 NAS).
4) Do not get anyone else involved unless they are part of the problem or part of the answer. This closes the door to busybodies, gossip and slander.
5) Try to settle the conflict first between you and the other person alone, before getting others involved, following the procedure in Matt. 18:15-18.
6) Put first things first. Conflict resolution, according to Jesus, comes before worship and sacrifice (Matt. 5:23-24).
7) Before, during and after conflict, exercise a forgiving spirit.

Spiritual Dermatitis (Thin Skin)

There were two ladies in the Philippian church who apparently were having a hard time getting along. Their names were Euodias and Syntche (Phil. 4:2). A preacher friend of mine jokingly renamed them "You-are-odious" and "Soon-touchy." You-are-odious was always offending people and Soon-touchy was the one who was always taking offense.

Most of us have met people on these two extremes in the life of the church. Obviously, we don't want to be like our friend You-are-odious. Jesus said, "Woe to him through whom they [offenses] come" (Luke 17:1 NAS). We read throughout the Bible that we are to take great pains not to offend anyone's conscience, customs or culture. It is with the other lady, Soon-touchy, that we will deal with here.

Soon-touchy is the hyper-sensitive person who gets wounded at the slightest negative comment (intentional or otherwise). She often allows this to cause her ministry, her marriage or her friendship to be sunk by the torpedo of what Jesus called a "stumbling block."

I purposely use the word "allows" because the degree to which she stumbles is to a great degree under her control. She has allowed spiritual dermatitis to spread in her life because she has *chosen* to get offended at the stumbling blocks in her path. Is it possible to condition our spiritual skin to be a little tougher, a little thicker and thereby less likely to develop irritation at the slightest contact with things that could offend us? I believe it is.

There is a common medical condition called "contact dermatitus." This is an inflammation of the skin where it has had contact with an outside irritant like poison ivy. The skin then becomes red and itchy, sometimes even developing blisters. The rub comes (no pun intended) when we scratch the irritation; the contact spreads and the condition gets worse. The parallel with our "spiritual skin" is obvious. We can choose to scratch the affected area and spread the problem or we can choose *not* to scratch it and it will heal.

Luke 17:1-10 contains four seemingly unrelated topics, the last of which is the parable of the unprofitable servant. In the first two verses, Jesus teaches us not to offend people and gives us a stern warning of what will happen if we do. The second two verses speak of the need for us to forgive others who offend or trespass against us. The third two verses are an exhortation to greater faith. Then follows the story of the unprofitable servant with Jesus asking three rhetorical questions in verses 7-9 and giving the obvious answer in verse 10.

Without going into too much detail, the point of the parable is this: a slave has no rights. He has been purchased by his master and is expected to do his job without any compensation. He expects nothing, he receives nothing. Even when he has done everything that was commanded him, he is called an "unprofitable servant" (vs.10).

Could it be that Jesus gave this parable to teach us the value of a *low* self-esteem so that we would not take offense so easily? This,

I realize contradicts much modern psychology, but seems to tie the four subjects in our passage together. It seems if our faith was increased (vs. 5,6) to really see our true status as unworthy slaves before God and man we would be much slower to give offense (vs. 1,2) and much quicker to forgive offenses (vs. 3,4).

It doesn't take a Greek scholar to notice that the Bible doesn't give a very flattering description of self. It tells us to deny self, die to self, crucify self, disdain selfish ambition and that the essence of sin is to follow our own selfish way. D.L. Moody once said, "My worst enemy is D.L. Moody." Was he schizophrenic, or was he simply describing the war within that has waged inside every believer since Paul wrote about his inner struggle in Romans 7?

Of course, we need to have a healthy view of ourselves and our value to God. However, this is because we're made in God's image and redeemed by Christ's precious blood, not because we're so special in and of ourselves.

Jesus said it was "inevitable" that offenses would come, and they will. The question is not whether or not it was intentional, who it was from or whether or not you deserved it, but rather how will you respond to it. Will you be "Soon-touchy," claiming your "right" to be treated fairly and squarely in an unfair world or will you give up your rights, because in reality you have none. You are a slave (and an unworthy one at that) with no rights, but a responsibility to follow Christ's example to exercise forgiveness and love when you are offended.

So the next time someone puts a stumbling block in your path, call to your memory a few things:

1) The offense has probably come because you are thinking more highly of yourself than you ought (Rom. 12:3).

2) The only time "self" and "esteem" are mentioned in the same passage in the Bible is when we are told to esteem others better than ourselves (Phil. 2).

3) If the offense was unintentional, give the person the benefit of the doubt and don't let it get "under your skin." If it does, then in humility inform the person of their

fault so they can see it, turn from it, learn from it and be restored (Gal. 6:1).

4) If the offense was intentional, make the choice to not let it ruin your day (or your life!). Don't give them the satisfaction of causing you to stumble in *your* walk with the Lord because of *their* sin.

Before you read on, take some time to examine your life for "stumbling blocks." Have you allowed someone or something from outside to knock you off course in your God-ordained testing? If so, forgive where necessary, lovingly confront when needed, and ask God for a thicker layer of skin to help avoid the consequences of spiritual dermatitus in the future.

Likewise patients who regularly get a physical exam as a check-up on their health, so we should do a spiritual check-up looking for the symptoms of the maladies that, if left untreated, will surely quench our zeal for God.

Stoker quote

"Don't worry about how to get a crowd to preach to. Just go out and catch fire and people will come to watch you burn."

John Wesley

Chapter Eight

Do Something

"...Jesus Christ; who gave himself for us, that he might redeem us from all iniquity, and purify unto himself a peculiar people, zealous of good works."
Titus 2:14 (KJV)

The man who has most singularly influenced the world for evil in the 20th century became a "man obsessed" because of two tragic incidents in his youth. At age 16, Vladimir Ulinov overheard a priest advise his father to beat him into submission if he didn't go to church. About the same time Vladimir witnessed the hanging of his older brother, who was wrongfully convicted of treason.

Driven by a bitter hatred of God, the church, government, and other authorities, the young Russian embraced Marxist-atheist ideology and fomented a revolution that spread like a cancer around the world. It was said of this man called Lenin that he dreamed of revolution 24 hours a day. He had a cause and dove into it with utter abandon.

I sometimes wonder what might have happened if a loving Christian friend had gotten hold of young Vladimir and turned him in the right direction. What if his revolutionary dreams could have been channeled into the cause of evangelizing the world? What if his desire for communist world domination driven by hatred could have been replaced by burning love for God and His Kingdom? Only God knows.

We cannot change history, but we can learn from it. We can be healers and friends to those whose wounds drive them into false ideologies and self-destructive passions. We can further resolve to be more stoked about our awesome, life-giving God and His Kingdom, than those who foment counterfeit ideologies like communism.

The verse above points out that God wants us to be a people who are zealous for good works. God would have us be boiling hot *to do* his work.

Charles Spurgeon said, "While committees waste their time over resolutions, do something. While Societies and Unions are making constitutions, let us win souls. Too often we discuss, and discuss and discuss and Satan laughs in his sleeve."[1]

Zealous for Good Deeds

There is a great illustration from the Civil War about the importance of "doing" that those of us in God's army can learn from. The great Confederate General Stonewall Jackson was moving his troops through Virginia when their progress was blocked by a river. Jackson gave orders to build a bridge. He awoke the next morning to see a crude-looking pile of rocks, logs and other debris that, ugly as it was, would enable his army to cross the river. As he mounted his horse, the General asked one of his lieutenants, "Where are the engineers?" The lieutenants replied, "They are in the tent drawing up plans to build the bridge!"[2]

We in the church are often like the engineers, constantly planning to do but doing very little. The early church was full of activists

---

1. Charles Spurgeon, *Lectures to My Students.*
2. Norm Lewis, *Priority One, What God Wants* (Promise Publishing) 16.

and spiritual radicals who were ready and willing "to do," not just talk about it. Those early zealots were accused of "turning the world upside down" as they moved out with unquenchable zeal to heal the sick, preach the Gospel and cast out demons. Their faith was no cerebral pursuit of theological knowledge but a fuel for the soul that ignited their whole being to action.

God's "Poema" and Plan

> *"For we are God's workmanship, created in Christ Jesus to do good works, which God prepared in advance for us to do"* (Eph 2:10 NIV).

An often-quoted cliche in Christian circles is that "God has a wonderful plan for your life." Unfortunately, cliches, even if they are true, lose their impact simply because they are so familiar. I'd like to make this next section as personal as I can. Do *you* believe that God has a specific, detailed, wonderful plan for your life? Do *you* believe that He not only cares, but plans in advance where He wants you to go, what He wants you to do and who you are to do it with?

Ephesians 2:10 shows that "in advance" God has ordained good works for us to do. Coupled with our opening verse in Titus 2:14, we can conclude that God wants us to be zealous (stoked) to do certain good works (not just any good works), that He has specifically planned for us.

I've heard some Christian teachers say there are various "wills" of God that could be acceptable to Him and the important thing is not that we would find God's will but that we would learn how to make good decisions based on our knowledge of God and the Bible. While it is true that many of our decisions in life are made in this way, I believe that something as important as our calling in life is important to our heavenly Father.

We are not only to be led by the Bible, but led by the Spirit. I suppose that technically anything that God allows is His "permissive" will, but we are told to prove what is "the good, and acceptable and perfect will of God" (Rom 12:2). This indicates there is a "perfect will of God."

The word "workmanship" in Eph. 2:10 comes from the Greek word *poema* which means a "work of art." From it we get our English word poem. We are God's "work of art," a beautifully crafted masterpiece. God doesn't make any junk, and that's especially true of us homo sapiens, the highest of form of flesh in His creation. We are created in His image to reflect His glory in a dark world through the good works He's called us to do.

Since He created us for these good works, we must have a servant's attitude as we go about them. Keep in mind Jesus' parable of the unprofitable servant (Luke 17:7-10). We must first prove to be faithful in what He gives us to do now, before He gives us more responsibility and authority in ministry.

Greg Laurie, who pastors one of America's largest churches and has won thousands to Christ through his Harvest Crusades, got his start in ministry in an interesting way. When he volunteered to serve his church, his pastor, Chuck Smith, sent him out to pick up cigarette butts in the church parking lot. One reason Greg was able to obey so easily is because he had seen Chuck's model of leadership by servanthood.

Before his Calvary Chapel exploded in size, Chuck pastored a string of small churches in the southwest. In that capacity he taught the Bible, fixed clogged toilets, jump-started cars, and served his congregations in countless other ways.

Smith Wigglesworth was a healing evangelist in the early part of this century. He began by being faithful as a plumber in England. Soon he was not only fixing people's pipes, but their souls and bodies and his ministry was released. William Carey, the pioneer missionary to India, started as a shoemaker. Hudson Taylor, who opened inland China to Christ, first served as a pharmacist's helper. C.T. Studd, the Michael Jordan of English cricket, went on to found the Heart of Africa Mission after proving faithful in his career as an athlete.

Unfortunately, many people sit around waiting for a lightning bolt or an audible voice from God before they'll get moving for the Lord. Even if you don't have God's total blueprint for your life (and few of us do), simply look for a place to serve and do it!

It's often while we're serving that God opens up other doors for ministry. Happy is the person who finds his center of gravity where he is right now. If you're one of those horizon-gazers who is so troubled about the future that you can't be happy in the present, remember what Jesus said about "taking no thought about tomorrow" (Matt. 6:34). God wants us to live in the present, and from there, He'll happily guide you into the future. Keep in mind that it's *His* plan for our lives. To discover our destiny we must first realize *Who* it is that has destined us to get there.

Five Finger Guidance

In determining God's will for a particular decision or determining future guidance, I use a simple procedure. I put my hand in front of me and check off five Scriptural ways of determining the will of God.

1. Our Desires—

> *"Delight yourself in the Lord; and He will give you the desires of your heart"* (Ps. 37:4 NAS).

As we serve God and delight ourselves in Him, often His desires become one with ours. I believe that often when a sincere Christian is on his knees, beating his breast to find God's will, the Lord will simply want to tap him on the shoulder and say, "What do *you* want to do?"

This happened once to me with one of the biggest decisions I made in my life. I was fasting and praying about the future for my wife and I and our new baby. I was walking on the beach and looked up to the sky and said in exasperation, "God, what do you want me to do?" Immediately I heard the Spirit speak to my heart. "What do you want to do?" A millisecond later I responded, "I want to evangelize and train others to evangelize." Then, as clear as a bell I heard, "Then why don't you join YWAM?" I had heard of this group before, but didn't know much about it. After a little fact-finding, my wife and I were off to our destiny and have been evangelizing and training others for over 15 years.

Not all of my guidance decisions have come that easily, but often God wants to "reward those who diligently seek Him" (Heb. 11:6), by giving us the very desires of our heart. I can honestly say I would rather be doing what I'm doing now than anything else in the world. I'm doing what I want to do, but the fact is that God gave me *His* desires as I sought His will.

2. The Written Word of God—

> "*Thy word is a lamp unto my feet, and a light unto my path*" (Ps. 119:105 KJV).

The Bible, and the principles given to us in the Bible, are not only the direct source of much of our guidance, but the standard by which we judge *all* guidance. As Christians we must give more than lip service to the statement that, "All scripture is inspired by God and profitable for teaching, for reproof, for correction, and for training in righteousness" (2 Tim. 3:16 RSV). A constant diet of God's word will take out many of the potholes on the road to God's will.

The missionary training center that I oversee is committed to the fulfillment of the Great Commission commandment to "make disciples of all nations..." by "...teaching them to obey all things whatsoever I have commanded you..." (Matt. 28:19,20). Therefore our strategy for where we go and what we do when we get there is always seen through the grid of the Great Commission. We are to make disciples, not just decisions. We are to go to *all* nations, therefore high priority is given to those who have never heard. We are to teach them to obey Jesus' commands, therefore church planting and discipleship hold equal importance with evangelism in our strategy.

Any missionary strategy that does not fulfill the above commands is called into question. Being ruthlessly biblical in all we do will save us from the road to ruin that is the end for him who does not esteem God's Word "...more than my necessary food" (Job 23:12).

3. The Spoken Word of God—

> "*Faith comes by hearing, and hearing by the word of God*" (Rom. 10:17 NKJV).

We know the entire Christian life is to be lived by faith. "For we walk by faith, not by sight...Without faith it is impossible to please God" (2 Cor. 5:7 KJV, Heb. 11:6 NIV). Faith comes by hearing. Therefore, we must endeavor to "hear" the word of the Lord to us individually as well as the written word of God in the Bible. What we believe to be God's "still small voice" (1 Kings 19:12) must, of course, not contradict biblical truths. We must also realize there are many things the Bible does not tell us. For instance, we are told to, "Go into all the world..." (Matt. 16:15), but the Bible doesn't tell us where we *individually* are supposed to go. Marriage is ordained by God, but we are not told in the Bible *who* we are to marry or indeed if we're to marry at all.

Many Christians are afraid to trust God's spoken word because of false prophets like Joseph Smith, Jim Jones or David Koresh, all of whom claimed to hear from God. The subjective nature of the spiritual realm scares some into a safe posture of "Bible and brain" guidance, that is, "You've got a Bible and a brain; figure out God's will and go for it."

Yes, let's be careful—but let's not throw the baby out with the bathwater. The Holy Spirit is the Third Person in the Holy Trinity. Let's honor Him as God, trust Him to guide us and "speak" to us. "If ye then, being evil, know how to give good gifts unto your children: how much more shall your heavenly Father give the Holy Spirit to them that ask him?" (Luke 11:13 KJV).

4. The Counsel of Others–

"Where no counsel is, the people fall: but in the multitude of counsellors there is safety"
(Prov. 11:14 KJV).

Often in God's plan we'll get by with a little help from our friends. He has placed members in His Body the same way He has constructed the human body, where the members care for each other (1 Cor. 12:25). When we seek counsel from others we are not only expressing humility and dependence on others, but we are availing ourselves of wisdom and safety that can only come from a multitude of counsellors.

Consider this illustration: You have four people sitting around a globe describing the world to a blind man. One sees only the Pacific Ocean; another sees only Asia. Opposite them are one who sees only the Atlantic and Americas; and another who sees just Europe and Africa. Only when all four describe what they see, can the blind man get a true picture of what the world looks like.

So it is with counsel. Our friends, co-workers, parents and leaders can often give us a more objective viewpoint on our situation. Because they are watching it from a distance, they are able to see what we cannot, and thereby provide safety for us as we make a decision.

Whenever you are facing a major decision (and sometimes minor ones), it is wise to seek godly counsel. I have been saved much pain and frustration in my life when I have had the good sense to ask someone else's opinion on a situation I was in. Some Christian friends may readily offer their counsel, but with others we need to aggressively seek it. "Counsel in the heart of man is like deep water; but a man of understanding will draw it out" (Prov. 20:5 KJV). We must be careful, of course, not to "walk in the counsel of the ungodly" (Ps. 1:1), or to give others such authority that they run our lives for us. Ultimately, God holds us responsible for the decisions we make.

5. Circumstances—

"A prudent man sees danger and takes refuge, but the simple keep going and suffer for it" (Prov. 22:3 NIV).

A fifth way of finding God's plan for our lives is simply to look at the circumstances we find ourselves in at the time. Solomon tells us that, "Wisdom calls aloud in the street..." (Prov. 1:20). We should always, when facing a decision, be aware of our surroundings and the circumstances we are providentially in at the time. Keep in mind that "The steps of a good man are ordered by the Lord" (Ps. 37:23 KJV); and often the very situation we are in will help us determine our next step.

To walk completely by circumstances, of course, would not require any faith. Many non-Christians run their lives almost exclusively on the basis of what they can see. We are expected to walk by faith and not by sight (2 Cor. 5:7). What we can see, however, can often be an indication of doors that God is opening and a confirmation to the other ways of hearing His voice. Paul presumed that God wanted him to remain in Ephesus until Pentecost because "a great door for effective work has opened to me..." (1 Cor. 16:9 NIV).

Any of these five methods would be incomplete at best and dangerous at worst if taken by themselves without reference to the others. Our desires can be clouded by our flesh and fallen nature. The Bible gives the principles and standards by which all voices, desires, circumstances and counsel are to be tested, but is limited in that other methods are needed to *apply* the Biblical truth to our particular situation. Hearing God's voice is crucial, but it is possible to be deceived. In counsel is safety, but counsel alone makes you the instrument of other people's guidance and gives them authority beyond what God intends. Circumstances are a good check and balance, but alone we would have no need to trust in an invisible God.

God's Referee

As I check off the five fingers on my hand and go through these methods of guidance I turn my hand palm-down parallel to the ground and place the index finger of my hand in the middle of the palm pointing vertical. This represents a sixth and final balancing factor—the peace of God.

Paul exhorted us to "let the peace of God rule in your hearts" (Col. 3:15 KJV). The word "rule" means to let His peace be the "referee" in your heart. Just as a referee in a football game makes sure the game is played according to the rules, God's peace will rule in your soul when you've followed a righteous course in your decision-making.

I have often found that when my wife, Linda, and I are seeking guidance, her sense of inner peace—or lack of it—can be a good compass for determining whether a particular decision lines up with God's will. The Holy Spirit, working through her, will either confirm or deny that we're on the right track.

This spirit-led guidance is much different than trusting in our feelings. It involves a sensitivity to God that goes beyond our understanding or emotions. After having filled the five conditions we need to trust the Lord, being careful not to "lean on our own understanding" (Prov. 3:5) and wait on Him for His peace or lack thereof.

Zealous for Spiritual Gifts

"... forasmuch as ye are zealous of spiritual gifts,
seek that ye may excel to the edifying of the church"
(1 Cor. 14:12 KJV).

Another factor in finding God's will is to discover and exercise our spiritual gifts. Once we find out in general *what* we are called to do by our giftings, the *where* and *with whom* come more easily. Knowing our giftings also automatically negates a lot of other "good" things we could be doing. Likewise, our lack of giftings in certain areas is often a good indicator of what we're *not to do*.

The Bible teaches that every believer has gifts from God and should use them to minister the "manifold grace of God" (I Pet. 4:10). The word "manifest" here was used in classical Greek to describe a garment woven of various different colors. Peter used this word to describe God's grace. Different members of Christ's Body manifest the grace of God in "many colored" ways by using our various spiritual gifts.

Here is another area where many Christians are frozen in waiting before they "do something." I've met people who seem to be stuck in a time warp waiting for a return to Pentecost, Azusa Street or the Jesus Movement. They're still seeking for their spiritual gifts, as if they were some mystical attainment of power. Their unearthly pursuit of "the gifts" makes them seem like the spiritual equivalent of an astrological sign.

Nothing could be further from the truth. God's gifts are spiritual, but practical. Supernatural, but used in the natural. They come from Heaven to be used on Earth. They are not a merit badge of spirituality, but divinely inspired equipment to serve people. They show God's many-colored grace to others in practical ways.

Our spiritual gifts are also the sunglasses through which you view the world and your service for the Lord. They usually bring us much joy and fulfilment. You'll be "stoked" when you are operating in your spiritual gifts because you'll know they are not your natural abilities. They are gifts of God's grace.

Of course, it's critical to remember that others are not looking through the same sunglasses. Both natural and spiritual giftings within the Church are all quite different, but God intends them to complement one another. Wise is the person who recognizes this, and draws on the giftings of others to compliment his/her own. Hippocrates understood this more than 2,300 years ago when he came up with his four temperament types. Churches, businesses and even the military have finally caught on to the fact that the whole will be more productive when they capitalize on the strengths of the individuals.

There are now many good books on spiritual gifts[3] and multitudes of personality tests and motivational analyses that can help you discern your giftings. I will not attempt to add to them. I simply would like to make a few distinctions in the various "species" of spiritual gifts.

Motivational Gifts

In Romans 12:6-8 there are seven gifts mentioned that are commonly referred to as "motivational" gifts. They are the outworking of who we are and how God created us to function. For instance, one of these gifts is leadership. Some people are made to be leaders. Some are not. The leader is told to "lead with diligence" (Rom. 12:8). Paul assumes they have the ability to lead so he urged them to be diligent or zealous about their role as a leader.

Your motivational gifts are at the core of who you are and how you express what God has put within you. You can enhance and develop such a gift, but God has to place the initial deposit there. An acquaintance of mine got a pointed example of this when he was

---

3. C. Peter Wagner, *Your Spiritual Gifts Can Help Your Church Grow*; Donald Gee, *The Gifts of the Spirit.*

going to Bible school in the Deep South. One day in the supermarket, the checkout lady presumed he was a student and asked what courses he was taking. "I'm studying to be a preacher," the young man replied. She lovingly looked over the rim of her glasses and remarked, "Honey, you don't study to be a preacher, you either is one or you ain't."

Here lies the value in discovering what makes you tick. What stokes you? As you begin to minister out of that gifting, God will show Himself to others through you.

I once heard the following illustration about motivational gifts: A hostess at a tea party trips and falls while bringing in a platter of tea cups to her guests. Immediately various gifts spring into operation. The prophetic person announces there has been an accident. The leader takes charge, sending others to get a broom, dustpan, mops, etc. The exhorter begins to encourage the embarrassed woman. The teacher finds the cause of the fall—an unseen step into the room—and instructs her on how not to fall again. The mercy-giver comforts the woman, the giver hands $50 to the woman to buy more teacups while the server cleans up the mess.

There wasn't time in the story for everyone to sit down and contemplate their response to the accident. They just responded according to who they were and how God made them. They were inwardly motivated to respond in a certain way and were all contributing to what needed to be done. The many parts of the Body were responding to a need.

Motivational gifts are some of the easiest to discover because all you have to do is observe your own behavior when you have opportunity to serve. As you begin by just "doing something," soon the doing becomes more detailed and specific. Peter tells us to "make our calling and election sure" (2 Peter 1:10). As we serve whenever we have opportunity, pretty soon we begin to "click" into what motivates us from above and within, much like gears on a car or bike. Our vehicle then begins to function more effectively. I would even go so far as to say that sometimes our gifts are discerned by "accident" as we decide to get going and "do something."

Manifestation Gifts

"Now to each one the manifestation of the Spirit is given for the common good" (1 Cor. 12:7 NIV).

In his first letter to the Corinthians, Paul mentions nine more gifts that build up the Body of Christ. I've chosen to call them "manifestation" gifts because they seem to pop up and manifest themselves when needed and otherwise are not seen. This is in contrast to the motivational gifts that seem to be part of our actual personality and an outworking of who we are. These gifts are more like tools that we carry in a spiritual toolbox. When an occasion arises where the Holy Spirit's workings need to be manifested, then we pull one of the tools out of the box and use it. When the need is met, the tool goes back into the box until the next time a manifestation of God's grace is needed.

The nine manifestation gifts are further broken down into three categories. First there are the "revelation" gifts—word of wisdom, word of knowledge and distinguishing of spirits. Revelational knowledge and wisdom from God comes to us as the need arises. Secondly, there are the "power" gifts—faith, gifts of healings and working of miracles. These are abilities to manifest supernatural faith and power from God to those in need. Then there are "speaking" gifts—prophesy, tongues and interpretation of tongues. This involves speaking supernaturally inspired words to build up those who hear them.

Using any of these nine gifts may seem a little scary at first because they require us to exercise faith and move into the supernatural. But they can become a natural part of any believer's spiritual life. The most important requirement is a desire to be used by God. Are you a willing vessel for His Spirit? Will you allow Him to manifest Himself through you to minister to others? Paul told us to "eagerly desire spiritual gifts…" (1 Cor. 14:1). We should ask God to make us zealous for the gifts, then diligently seek opportunities to move in them.

If you are not moving in spiritual power, perhaps it is because you don't want it enough. Perhaps you are satisfied with the "Bible and brain" method for living the Christian life. Or perhaps you're just afraid of the embarrassment if you step out in faith and it "doesn't work."

If this is the case, then perhaps God is waiting for you to see the futility of doing divine work with human ability. Maybe He's waiting for you to get desperate enough. Remember, He rewards those who diligently seek Him and gives His Holy Spirit to those who ask Him (Heb. 11:6, Luke 11:13). We'll never know how much God can use us if we don't take that first step of faith.

Once, as a young Christian leader, I was asked to pray for a little girl who was burning up with fever. Without an immediate healing she could die. Inwardly I started to panic. "What if she doesn't get healed?" I reasoned. But then I thought, "What if she does? You'll never know until you pray. Even if she doesn't get healed, she'll be no worse off than before you prayed." I laid hands on the girl's red-hot forehead and simply believed for her healing. As I began to pray, God stirred in me the gift of faith and she was healed. I can explain it no other way.

Another time I was in a prayer meeting with a group of leaders who were seeking to buy a radio station. We had put $80,000 down, but no other funds had come in. A deadline was approaching, and we were in danger of losing both the station and the $80,000. The room seemed to reek with unbelief and despair as one brother prayed one of those, "If it be thy will for us to go under..." prayers. All of a sudden I felt a surge of both anger and faith. I rose and said, "I do not believe it is God's will for us to lose the money or the station." I asked the pastor for permission to lead the group in a prayer of faith. As I did, we were stirred to a new level of faith and unity, and God came through! That station has since broadcast the message of Jesus almost continuously, touching many thousands of lives.

From this story, it may seem like I was "God's man of faith and power for the hour," but in reality I was as full of unbelief as anyone else in the room. Then a gift was manifested and God chose to give it to me. He gives gifts "to each just as he determines" (1 Cor. 12:11). Here lies the glory of the spiritual gifts. Like salvation, we don't deserve or earn them. He gives us the privilege of being channels through which He can manifest His glory to the world.

Ministry Gifts

> *"And He Himself gave some to be apostles, some prophets, some evangelists, and some pastors and teachers, for the equipping of the saints for the work of the ministry"* (Eph. 4:11-12 NKJV).

The ministry[4] gifts are the leadership gifts in the Body of Christ. As stated in this Scripture, they are the means God has chosen to equip His people for works of service. They were given upon Christ's ascension as a key resource to continue the work He left behind.

Unfortunately, many Christians have misunderstood God's intentions for how these roles were to function in the church. One of the most devastating doctrines to enter the church is the clergy-laity system. This is the belief that an elite group called priests, pastors or ministers are chosen by God to do His "spiritual" work, while the rest of us do the "secular" work. This thinking casts us into heavyweight and lightweight divisions in the boxing match against the devil. And nothing could be further from the truth.

First of all, there is no real secular-sacred dichotomy. All believers are priests and therefore ministers of God (1 Peter 2:9, Rev. 5:10). Secondly, even if the five leadership gifts mentioned above were in an elite "clergy" category, their primary job is to equip the rest of us to do "the ministry." So for them to be called ministers in the true biblical sense, they need to be releasing others into ministry.

It doesn't take long to discover if you have a leadership or ministry gift. Godly leadership has some unmistakable characteristics. It is born out of faith and obedience, and it seeks to serve and release others to fulfill their calling in God. We don't need a committee, a

---

4. Technically all spiritual gifts are ministry gifts in that they are given to enable us to serve others. These leadership gifts, however, are specific ministers who are gifts themselves to equip others in their ministry.

church council or a letter from the Pope or Billy Graham to confirm a leadership call. God himself confirms it. A church or ministry simply recognizes what He has already birthed in a man or woman's heart. That's why Hebrews 5:4 says, "No man takes this honor unto himself, but he that is called of God…"

Even with a leadership calling, it may take years to gain the depth of character and wisdom needed for some level of ministry. Jesus had his 30 years of preparation and Moses his 40. David had his sojourn with the sheep and Paul his devotion in the desert. I meet many young people who aspire to leadership, which is an honorable ambition (1 Tim. 3:1), but who are not willing to pay their dues. When God calls a man or a woman to lead, there will be times of pressure and preparation for the task ahead.

The amazing thing about these gifts of spiritual leadership is that God calls them forth in people who seemingly have no natural leadership giftings. Before I became a Christian, my only leadership role was as co-captain of my high school track team—and that was because I was a fast runner, not a charismatic leader. After I became a believer, God suddenly began to draw out abilities I never knew I had. As I began doing the work of an evangelist, God began stirring others to join with me. As a result, within a year of my conversion, I often found myself in positions of leadership. I didn't seek leadership. I discovered my leadership gift while simply doing the work God called me to. Other leaders who recognized this gift in me, helped to cultivate it by mentoring me in the ways of God and modeling a lifestyle of servant leadership.

As leaders, our role (apostolic, prophetic, evangelistic, pastoral or teaching) and our rule ("…rulers of thousands, hundreds, fifties and tens") must be determined by the Lord. We would be well advised to stay in the "sphere" of leadership God has gifted us for. A leadership gift is both a great privilege and a great responsibility. The gifts are not for ourselves, but for God's purposes in serving and equipping others to do the work of the ministry.

Just Do It!

Do is the biggest little word in the Bible. It separates the armchair theologians from the world-changers. The pleasure cruisers

from the battleships. The wallflowers from the dancers. The specta-
tors from the players, the.... OK, I'll stop! You get the point. God
has commissioned every one of us to help extend His Kingdom.
That means believers need to "get the lead out" and get moving into
God's destiny for their lives.

If God has identified your spiritual gifts, then start functioning
in them. If you're still seeking God's will or an understanding of
your giftings, *do* what you can with what you've got to glorify Him
by serving others.

There are two types of transgressions—sins of commission
(doing what we shouldn't)—and sins of omission (not doing what
we should). Both are lethal and are guaranteed to cut us off from a
lifestyle of real zeal.

I urge you today to make a decision to "Do not merely listen to
the word.... Do what it says" (Jas. 1:22 NIV). Jesus said, "Blessed rather
are those who hear the word of God and obey it" (Luke 11:28 NIV).

Do you have a hunger for the Word and a desire to impart it to
others? Then begin teaching and see what God will do. Do you have
a desire to win souls and see others do the same? Then evangelize
and see what God will do. Do you have a desire to see churches
planted here or overseas? Then go for it and see what God will do.
Do you think God is calling you to be an elder? Then "eld" and see
what God will do!

Stoker quote

"Revival is divine intervention in the normal course of spiritual things. It is God revealing Himself to man in awesome holiness and irresistible power. It is such a manifest working of God that human personalities are overshadowed and human programs abandoned. It is man retiring into the background because God has taken the field."

Arthur Wallis

Chapter Nine

Revival Fire

"...O, Lord, revive thy work in the midst of the years, in the midst of the years make known; in wrath remember mercy."
Habakkuk 3:2 (KJV)

In the mid-1800s, America found herself in deep spiritual trouble. The fires of the "Great Awakening" under Jonathan Edwards and George Whitefield (1735-1742) had long since burned out, and the church was having little impact on society.

Vices like greed, political corruption, sexual immorality, drunkenness, brawling and gambling became entrenched in the still young nation. Atheism, agnosticism and the occult were on the rise throughout the world, while apathy and indifference reigned in the American church. An economic crash that followed seemed to be a sign of God's judgment on the nation. Banks closed, railroads went bankrupt and unemployment soared. The call to faith and holy living that was so clear during the Awakening had been silenced by three generations of hearing without doing.

As businessman Jeremiah Lamphier walked the streets of New York, he was grieved by the spiritual and social devastation he saw. In 1857, he decided to do something about it. He gave up his business to work as a street evangelist. Lamphier believed prayer was a key to revival, and began passing out flyers advertising a Wednesday noontime prayer meeting at the Dutch Church on Fulton Street. When Wednesday noon came, no one showed up. Lamphier's faith was tested as the minutes ticked by. He was sure God had called this prayer meeting. So where were the people?

At 12:30, six men arrived, and they began to pray. The next week, 20 people came to the meeting, and the group soon decided to meet daily. Within six months, over 10,000 businessmen were meeting every day, crying out to God for revival. These prayer meetings were held in stores, homes, company buildings and churches, and the participants came from many Christian denominations. Prayer united their hearts and quickly overshadowed doctrinal differences.

The results were staggering. Within two years over a million converts were added to U.S. churches. A return to biblical values sparked social and ethical changes that continued for 50 years. The fire leaped across the Atlantic to Great Britain where another million souls joined the churches. It was such a powerful move of God that it was dubbed "The Second Great Awakening" by J. Edwin Orr, arguably the world's foremost authority on revival.

Many of Christianity's greatest leaders were launched out of this second revival. People like D. L. Moody, Hudson Taylor, Andrew Murray, F. B. Meyer, R. A. Torrey, A. B. Simpson and William and Catherine Booth to name a few. However, it's interesting to note that the initial spark for this great revival came from an unknown businessman named Jeremiah Lamphier. He was the "catalyst" for what was to come.

The Catalyst

J. Edwin Orr has devoted his life to the subject of revival, and his teaching tapes list four characteristics that are common to the hundreds of revivals he has studied:

1. Extraordinary prayer.
2. Conviction of sin—in the church and among its leaders.
3. Effective evangelism—an ingathering of lost souls.
4. Social change.

Orr points out that these characteristics are almost always evident and *in that order*. Changes in society happen because of radical changes in the hearts of individuals who have been born-again. These new believers were drawn in by the Spirit of God, who was also dealing with the sin in the church because of fervent prayer.

It is, of course, God who pours out His "Spirit of grace and supplication" (Zech. 12:10) on His people, but the people must respond. There is usually a catalyst—a person or persons willing to intercede through fervent, prevailing prayer. Someone needs to "stand in the gap" (Ezek. 22:30) for the people.

A generation after the Second Great Awakening, the coals of revival again began to lose their glow. A young college student named Evan Roberts, who had begun working in a Welsh coal mine to support himself, turned out to be God's catalyst for the next move of God. One day at work an explosion ripped through the coal mine. Evan was unharmed, but found his Bible had been damaged. The page that was burned was 2 Chronicles 6—where a young Solomon prays for revival!

Soon afterward, Evan Roberts began to fervently intercede for an awakening in Wales. He prayed so long and loud that his landlady evicted him, thinking that he was mad. After 13 months of "standing in the gap" for the nation, the Welsh Revival began and Evan's "scorched Bible" became legendary.

The revival struck Wales like a thunderbolt. Strong men wept under conviction of sin. Families were reunited. Whole neighborhoods were converted—and the Spirit of God seemed to set ablaze the whole nation. Young people got saved and stoked. Enthusiasm and fervor for holiness were high. Praise and worship reached new heights as crowds would gather nightly to worship the God who had visited them. Roberts was not a great preacher or even a pastor. Witnesses from the Revival say he would monitor the meetings as the Spirit moved among the people in prayers, songs and testimonies. He was God's catalyst.

Evan Roberts believed that the Welsh Revival was a fulfillment of Joel 2:28 regarding God's Spirit being poured out on all flesh in the last days. However, he believed "all flesh" must prepare to receive revival to experience it. He gave four conditions:

1. The past must be clean—every sin confessed to God, every wrong to man put right.
2. Everything doubtful removed from our lives. Any grey areas, away with them.
3. Obedience—prompt, implicit, unquestioning to God.
4. Public confession of Christ as Lord.

The fires of the Welsh Revival continued to burn for years, spreading to other nations and transforming hundreds of thousands of lives. It all started in the heart of a young man who was filled with compassion for a world with no one to weep over it.

Fire Begets Fire

There is probably no better metaphor than fire to describe the way revival starts and spreads. An arsonist with just a single match and a strong wind behind him can set the entire countryside ablaze. The wildfires that regularly sweep across Australia and parts of the United States during the dry season graphically depict the awesome power of a firestorm.

In a revival, God uses similar elements. First, there is the arsonist—the pyromaniac who lives to start fires. In our case, the fires are for salvation, not destruction. A spiritual arsonist is the best thing that can happen to a church or a city.

The fuel is the souls of men and women, so spiritually dry that the slightest spark of life will set them ablaze. Through prayer and evangelism, the pyromaniac sets them off with the fire of God. And the Holy Spirit, like a mighty wind, blows the flame into a raging inferno. How interesting that the wind-fed fires that horrify us in the natural are the very thing we seek in the spiritual realm.

Could it be that God wants to use you as a spiritual pyromaniac who'll ignite others with a passion for God? The answer is yes! Although revival is a sovereign act of God, it is clear from church history that He uses ordinary human instruments like us as His fire-starters. Some of the catalysts of revival I've mentioned—like Jeremiah Lamphier, Evan Roberts and Jonathan Edwards—were not great men by the world's standards. They were ordinary people with an uncompromising faith in a great God.

Many other fire-starters are not named in the pages of church history, but God used them all the same. I've heard many stories of obscure prayer warriors who cried out to God in secret. One example is the elderly ladies in Southern California who prayed for an awakening among the youth shortly before the Jesus Movement of the 1970s got moving. There are other accounts of school children who cried out to God for months prior to the outbreak of recent revivals in Argentina and Korea.[1]

Of course, God can use people in positions of authority too. Shortly after missionaries landed in Hawaii in 1820 the daughter of one of the most influential of the Hawaiian chiefs was converted. Recognizing the stronghold the pagan gods held over the people, High Chieftess Kapiolani took an entourage of followers and trekked up the slopes of Kilauea, the active volcano. She reached the ledge of the fiery pit and openly defied the powerful goddess of fire, Pele, in a confrontation similar to Elijah and the prophets of Baal. Pele did nothing.

Kapiolani's actions showed the Hawaiian people they did not have to fear the gods and set the stage for the revival to follow shortly thereafter. In the year she died, 1841, the largest church in the world was in Hilo, Hawaii, with over 6,400 members.

Since it's clear that God can use anyone as His fire-starter, the question now is: Are you available for God to use you? Will you be His torch-bearer, setting fires of revival in those around you?

---

1. See Edward Miller's *Thy God Reigns* and *Visions Beyond the Veil* for other examples.

God's Typos

Paul, who lit a fire in the heart of a young disciple named Timothy, would not be satisfied until Timothy was spreading that fire to others. One way it spread from Paul to others was by word of mouth. In 2 Tim. 2:2 (NIV), he says: "...the things you have heard me say in the presence of many witnesses entrust to reliable men who will also be qualified to teach others."

Another often underestimated and overlooked way of spreading the fire is by our example. Paul exhorted his young, timid, sickly disciple, "Don't let anyone look down on you because you are young, but set an example for the believers in speech, in life, in love, in faith and in purity" (1 Tim. 4:12 NIV).

The word example is from the Greek work "typos" from which we get our word "type," as in typewriter. It means "an impression left by a blow" or a "mark left from a beating," like a black eye. The same word is used to describe the nail prints in Jesus' hands (John 20:25). We are to leave such an impression on people by our example that it is the spiritual equivalent of giving them a black eye.

The operative word here is influence. Our godly example, by our attitudes and actions, is to ignite spiritual fire in others. Sometimes our influence is conscious, but often it is not. Jesus seemed to recognize the power of godly influence when He said, "Let your light so shine before men, that they may see your good works, and glorify your Father which is in Heaven" (Matt. 5:16 KJV). Paul told the Philippians that they were to be "blameless and harmless,...without fault in the midst of a crooked and perverse generation, among whom you shine as lights in the world" (Phil. 2:15 NKJV).

John Wesley, the founder of Methodism, was converted through the godly influence of Moravian missionaries who were traveling on the same ship from America to Europe. During the voyage, a storm arose that threatened the lives of all on board. While Wesley became frantic with fear, he was astonished to see that the Moravians were calmly singing praises to God. He questioned how they could be at peace at such a time, and they simply testified of their assurance of salvation.

Wesley later attended one of their meetings and was given a book written by Martin Luther. His heart was, as he described it, "strangely warmed," and he was saved and became a catalyst for revival in England. The Moravians and Luther were God's "typos."

In 1933, another group of God's typos began a prayer meeting that, over the next few decades, left the imprint of Jesus on millions of lives. It began when some businessmen in Charlotte, North Carolina, started praying together because of their concern over the spiritual decay there during the Depression.

They called for a day of fasting and prayer in the woods outside of Charlotte, and 29 men took part. The group invited evangelist Mordecai Ham to hold a tent-meeting in the city. One of his converts was a tall, skinny teenager who was to become another revival catalyst. His name was Billy Graham. The Billy Graham Association recently attributed at least 2 million conversions to his preaching. It all began with the influence of those few men.

Making an Impression for Jesus

I am often asked as I travel, "How can I be used by God to influence others for Christ? How can I really make a difference?" I'd like to suggest some ways you could be a catalyst for a move of God within your sphere of influence.

At the same time we received Jesus, we were given a new position of influence. Whether we realized it or not, we were commissioned as His ambassadors (2 Cor. 5:18-20) to the people we meet. When we identify ourselves with Jesus, people just naturally start observing us to see if our words and deeds line up with what they perceive as Christ-like characteristics. So recognizing this influence and using it effectively is the first step to becoming a good ambassador for Christ.

Many of us are like the Jimmy Stewart character in the classic movie "It's a Wonderful Life" in that we fail to recognize how much our lives impact others. Stewart played the role of George, a small town businessman who became suicidal because of mistakes he'd made. But before he could leap from the bridge, George encountered an angel, who replayed a short "video" of his life. The angel showed him how radically different his hometown would have been, if not for his positive influence. When George sees this, it gives him the courage to face his mistakes and to confront the town villain.

In my 15+ years of involvement in missionary training and evangelism, I've come to recognize that our actions speak at least as loud as our words when it comes to winning people to Christ. For several years, I have been polling people in churches, YWAM schools and other places on what they consider the primary factor in their decision to turn to Jesus.

These are the ten choices I give them:

1. God's love
2. God's wrath (fear of Hell)
3. Life after death (hope of Heaven)
4. Guilt over sin (awareness of need for forgiveness)
5. Godly parents
6. Godly influence of a Christian friend or acquaintance
7. Clear presentation of the Gospel (by evangelist, pastor or personal witness)
8. Well-reasoned arguments (apologetics)
9. Personal trauma (loss of spouse, fiancee, death of loved one, personal injury, etc.)
10. Godly church (fellowship)

Outside of those born into a Christian family, number six usually scores the highest percentage. That's a very good reason for us to be godly "living epistles" to our friends and neighbors.

An old sage once said, "I'd rather see a sermon any day than hear one." We need to occasionally consider what kind of sermon our friends see in us. For although an ambassador is expected to have a positive influence, his words and actions can have a negative one as well.

An elderly American Bible teacher I once met left a typo I will long remember. I was sitting in a Texas ice cream parlor with Gospel singer Keith Green (who helped stoke my fire for God) when this man unexpectedly joined us at our table. As we licked our ice cream cones, he ranted against several Christian groups. As he rattled on in a vindictive tone, the first thought that popped into my mind was, "I feel sorry for his poor wife!" I decided right then that was *not* how I wanted to end up in the latter years of my ministry.

By contrast, another man I met left a typo so positive that it greatly influenced the course of my life. In 1979, Linda and I were newly married and considering joining Youth With A Mission. While weighing the decision, I went on a YWAM short-term outreach to the South Pacific Games in Fiji. Part of my motive was to win souls, but part was to check out this organization. I told Linda, "I don't want to join up with a bunch of hot dogs!" In my earlier church involvment, I'd seen revival fires get snuffed by leaders who spent more time jockeying for position and power than praying and serving their people.

So in Fiji, it was refreshing to observe leaders who walked in humility and truly preferred one another. I particularly observed Dave Hall, a soft-spoken YWAM leader who left a "black eye" on me as I watched him serving and leading by example. He didn't realize it, but his typos helped fuel my evangelistic and missionary fire and seal my destiny in linking up with YWAM.

Author Gordon MacDonald lists five types of people who influence our passion for God. First there are the Very Resourceful People. These are our mentors and leaders—those who *ignite* our passion. Next are the Very Important People. These are our peers, our colleagues who *share* our passion. Third are the Very Trainable People. These are our "Timothys," those under our leadership in one way or another who *catch* our passion. Next are the Very Nice People. These are the ones whom we know at a distance, as the "multitudes" who followed Jesus. They *enjoy* our passion. The last group are the Very Draining People. These are those who bug us to death, but we nonetheless grit our teeth and "love them in the Lord." They *sap* our passion.[2]

As you read this last paragraph you probably had various folks come into your mind. My question to you is this: How do *you* affect the passion of others? Which type of person are you? How would others in your sphere of influence categorize you if they read this page? Let's hope you are on the positive side, igniting and fueling the fire of God in others.

---

2. Gordon MacDonald, *Restoring your Spiritual Passion* (Oliver-Nelson Books) 73.

Distribute Combustible Materials

Look for opportunities to spread revival fire by being a purveyor of flammable substances. By this I mean Christian literature that will ignite the heart of a person who has the least flicker of spiritual passion. Start by being a collector, then look for opportunities to distribute.

Since I came to faith in Christ, there have been various tapes and books that have influenced me greatly and stoked my fire for God. I have gotten into the habit of working deals with publishers, buying these materials in bulk and giving them away consistently as the Lord leads.

For instance, I was once struggling with a besetting sin and a friend recommended *How to Find Freedom from the Power of Sin* by T.A. Hegre. It helped me greatly, so I bought 20 of them and placed them in my stockpile of stokable materials. One night while street preaching, a man pulled me aside to talk. He confessed that he had been a Christian earlier in his life, but had given in to lust and had sunk back into sin. I sent him Hegre's book, and it helped turn his life around. Today he is in the ministry.

I was at the Christian Booksellers Convention a few years ago and bought, at great discount, 500 copies of two other books that have had tremendous influence on me—*Humility* by Andrew Murray, and *The Calvary Road* by Roy Hession. I have spent the last couple of years joyfully stoking other Christians' revival fire with these classics.

I've committed other acts of spiritual arson by giving *The Soul Winner* by Spurgeon to young evangelists; *The Best of Tozer* to those who needed a prophetic punch; Gordon MacDonald's *Ordering your Private World* for those who needed discipline; and E. M. Bound's books to those who needed instruction on prayer. Once I've given away a book that stoked my own fire, I sit back and giggle with satisfied glee as the flame spreads to them and starts raging out of control.

We should never undestimate the power of good Christian literature. Jonathan Goforth was a dissatisfied, disappointed and desperate missionary to China until someone gave him a copy of *Revival Lectures* by Charles Finney. Soon his life and ministry were revitalized as he put Finney's biblical principles to work. Subsequently, thousands were converted through his ministry.

Both Finney and Wesley's writings had tremendous influence on William and Catherine Booth as they founded the Salvation Army. Watergate "hatchet man" Charles Colson was converted when someone tossed a "Molotov cocktail" his way in the form of a book called *Mere Christianity* by C. S. Lewis. D. L. Moody was so convinced of the stoking power of the printed page that he started two publishing houses. My prayer is that by God's grace this very book will stoke thousands and the fire would spread.

Any good Christian bookstore will carry a variety of periodicals that make excellent blasting caps to help explode the reader into revival fire. I have listened to hundreds of audio teaching tapes and continue to do so when exercising, working, driving, taking a shower and other activities. When one of them is a real bell-ringer, I love to send it to friends and missionaries around the world. Teaching videos and Christian music tapes can also spread the fire.

The Prevailing Prayer

The volume of our voice and the length or intensity of our prayers are not necessarily the determining factor in whether they get answered. There is, however, something to be said for prevailing, fervent prayer. The apostle James used the example of Elijah (who prayed "earnestly") to illustrate to us that the "effectual fervent prayer of a righteous man availeth much" (Jas. 5:16-18).

There is prayer and then there is fervent prayer. The early Christians in Jerusalem prayed "earnestly" for Peter (Acts 12) while Paul told the Colossians that Epaphras was "laboring fervently" for them in prayer (Col. 4:12). In the context of spiritual warfare,[3] Paul exhorted the Ephesians to pray "with all *perseverance* and *supplication...*" (Eph. 6:18). God promises to reward the diligent seeker, not necessarily the casual inquirer.

---

3. Much has been written about spiritual warfare, and some of it gets off on complicated methods of fighting the principalities and powers that rule in the heavenlies. In the one passage of Scripture that actually illustrates this warfare, it is interesting that the "weapon" that Daniel used to break through satanic interference was simple, yet powerful prayer—with fasting (Daniel 9).

"You will seek me and find me when you seek me with all your heart" (Jer. 29:13 NIV).

Getting back to J. Edwin Orr's four marks of revival, number one on his list is "extraordinary prayer." As the world continues to plunge deeper into darkness, we need to put first things first. God needs prayer warriors to step out and lead others into extended sessions of fervent prayer for revival.

In the Vietnam War, platoons of U.S. soldiers often ventured out on foot into territory occupied by the Viet Cong. One man was always chosen as the "point man" who would lead the others into the eerie darkness of mine-infested, enemy-infiltrated jungle. The point man faces great danger and carries great responsibility, but he is essential for the successful penetration into enemy territory and eventual victory in the war.

God also needs point men and women to lead His soldiers into the front lines of battle. To use another war analogy, fervent intercessory prayer is like the preliminary bombing that "softens" the enemy before the ground troops can go in to actually possess the territory. Petra, the Christian rock group, has a line from one of their songs that says, "Get on your knees and fight like a man." Our nation and world cannot go on too much longer without a revival. We have no choice. We must fight. We must get on our knees and pray.

Begin in your own private prayer life. Cry out to God from "within the circle" for personal revival. Then pray with others for revival in your church and community. Promote half-nights of prayer, all-night prayer meetings or prayer retreats for the purpose of intercession for awakening in the church.[4] Learn how to fast and pray. Learn to pray when you don't feel like praying. Learn to pray by praying. Pass on combustible books that ignite a passion for prayer in the hearts of those who read. Read church history books on the awakenings of the past. Meditate on pertinent passages in the Bible regarding prayer. But above all—**PRAY.**

---

4. Be careful as you pray for the church not to slip into self-righteousness. As you pray let the sin, immorality and weakness in the church break and send you deeper into prayer. Otherwise it will be easy to get critical as you focus on the problems. Remember the first revival principle is "if my people will humble themselves" (2 Chron. 7:14).

Lighting the First Candle

In December of 1989, the Romanian communist government, led by ruthless dictator Nicolae Ceausescu, ordered the eviction of Pastor Lazlo Tokes from his home and church. Tokes and his family were to be forcibly moved to a village far from their home in the university town of Timisoara.

Just two years earlier, Pastor Tokes had assumed leadership of the Hungarian Reformed Church in Timisoara. At the time, the church had shrunk to fewer than 50 members, mostly old people left over from the tenure of the former pastor, a communist collaborator. Tokes immediately started Bible studies and baptized new converts. A "Jesus Movement" of sorts started as hundreds of young and old flocked to his church. He also worked for unity among the various Protestant, Orthodox and Catholic churches.

On Sunday, December 10, Pastor Tokes told his congregation that he was to be evicted on Friday because of his pastoral work. He asked them to come and be peaceful witnesses of the unlawful invasion of his civil rights. When the secret police showed up on December 15, the doors to the church were blocked by a human barricade. As the police tried to figure out what to do, hundreds more joined the protest.

Meanwhile, Daniel Gavra, a student and member of a Baptist Church made his way through the crowd towards his pastor, Peter Dugulesau. Peter was nervous as he saw a lump underneath the young student's jacket, thinking it was a weapon. Then, Daniel opened his jacket to reveal a packet with dozens of candle stubs.

At one in the morning, Pastor Tokes and his wife peered out their window to see hundreds of candles piercing the darkness. Hands, cupped close to the people's hearts, sheltered the flickering flames which lighted their faces with a warm glow.

Before dawn, the police forcefully broke through the human barricade. As Pastor Tokes held his Bible to his face, he was beaten bloody and taken away. The swelling crowds surged toward Timisoara's central square. The government responded by filling the streets with armed soldiers, dogs and tanks.

As Daniel Gavra and others distributed more candles to the chanting crowd, the troops opened fire. Hundreds were shot, but the people stood strong. Gavra, the Baptist, linked arms with a young Pentecostal girl who was shot and killed beside him. Seconds later, Daniel himself fell to the ground as bullets tore through his left leg. The central square was littered with blood-soaked bodies of the dead and wounded.

The massacre sent shock waves through the nation. Stories of the Christians' courage and unity stirred the hearts of the long-repressed Romanian people. And by Christmas Day, Ceausescu and his tyrannical regime had been toppled. Though the price was high, truth triumphed over lies. The good guys won.

A few days after Christmas, Daniel's pastor stopped by the hospital where he was recuperating from his wounds. A large bandage covered the stump where his left leg had been. Daniel's body was broken, but not his spirit. "Pastor," he said, "I don't mind so much the loss of my leg. After all, it was I who lit the first candle."[5]

How about you? Could God be preparing you to light the first candle of revival in your sphere of influence? Could it be that you are the catalyst God wants to use to detonate a spiritual chemical reaction in your town? Go for it! Do it! Light the first candle! Dare to be a Daniel!

---

5. Charles Colson, *The Body* (Word Publishing) 52-61.

Stoker quote:

"A burning heart will soon find room for a flaming tongue."

Charles Spurgeon

Chapter Ten

Apostolic Ambition

"It has always been my ambition to preach the gospel where Christ was not known..."
Rom. 15:20 (NIV)

Most great men and women of God share this driving ambition to present the Gospel to people who have never heard. They set ministry goals and relentlessly pursue them. British statesman Winston Churchill once said, "Never give up, never, never, ever give up." Two of my apostolic heroes are men who never, ever gave up in their ambitious endeavors for God's honor and glory. Their apostolic ambition carried them through fiery trials and drove them on to amazing feats of ministry. They are good role models for us today who seek to preach the Gospel where Christ is not known.

One of them was once a swearing, cocky British teenager who, while working as a shoemaker's apprentice, was caught in a lie and felt such shame that he repented and gave his life to Christ.

At that moment, God ignited a fire in the heart of that young man. He then stoked it with a copy of *Captain Cook's Voyages*. As William Carey read about the famous sailor's exploits, it set him thinking about young people like him all over the world who had no access to the Gospel.

Once that apostolic ambition was birthed in his heart, there was no stopping him. His hunger for the Bible led him to pursue studies in Latin, Hebrew and Greek. His passion for missions led him to write a book, challenging Christians to send out missionaries. His book sold like wildfire throughout the English-speaking world. He soon founded a "Society for the Propagation of the Gospel Among the Heathen," and sailed for India in 1793.

In India he had to overcome tremendous obstacles. First of all, as a preacher he was boring, even in English. He worked seven years before he won his first convert. Meanwhile, his family was plagued by financial woes and sickness. Within two years of their arrival, his first wife Dorothy died, as did two of his children. He too was wracked by bouts of fever that left him totally bald by age 21. If that weren't enough agony, his missionary partner deserted him to sell rum; his missionary community split; and much of his Bible translation work was destroyed in a fire. He daily endured rural India's diseased and unsanitary conditions and had to dodge alligators, snakes and Bengal tigers to go about his duties.

Through it all, he pursued his ambition to preach the Gospel where Christ was not known. He translated the Bible into Bengali, Oriya, Marathi, Hindi, Assamese and Sanskrit, and Scripture portions in 29 other Indian languages and dialects. He planted churches, founded a Bible college, started a publishing ministry and through his writings and example inspired thousands of others to become missionaries. William Carey came to be known as "The Father of Modern Missions." Toward the end of his life he said about his accomplishments: "I can plod, I can persevere in any definite pursuit. To this I owe everything."

Seventeen centuries before Carey lived a scrawny, hook-nosed, bald-headed Jew named Saul of Tarsus. His life and identity were built on the pursuit of intellectual and theological knowledge.

Shortly after the mass conversions in Jerusalem during Pentecost he occupied himself with "...breathing threats and murder against the disciples of the Lord..." (Acts 9:1 NKJV). He was apprehended by Jesus on the road to Damascus and the rest is history.

Probably no man endured more or accomplished more for Christ than the Apostle Paul. The book of Acts and his 13 epistles are full of information on his trials and triumphs. Listen to some of his Spirit-inspired statements about himself: "...chains and afflictions wait for me. But none of these things move me, neither count I my life dear unto myself, so that I may finish my race with joy...What are you doing weeping and breaking my heart? For I am ready not only to be bound, but even to die in Jerusalem for the name of the Lord Jesus...For me to live is Christ and to die is gain... For I will gladly spend and be expended for you...I am the least of the apostles... but I labored more abundantly than they all, yet not I but the grace of God that was with me."

Then at the end of his life, he could confidently assert, "I have fought the good fight. I have kept the faith..." (2 Tim. 4:7 NKJV).

Have you ever read statements by guys like these and wondered how they did it? What motivated that kind of perseverance? And what fuel stoked their apostolic fire?

I believe it is the quality of ambition. Our English word ambition comes from a Latin word meaning "canvassing for promotion." It is the desire for fame, honor and excellence. The Bible[1] warns against selfish pursuit of such things. But ambition for God's glory is not only commendable but a divine command.

Paul had a consuming desire to glorify God. He knew the best way to accomplish that was to love Him and keep His commandments (John 14:15,21). He also knew that the last commandment Jesus gave us was to go and make disciples of all the nations (Matt. 28:18-20). This led him to proclaim to the Corinthians his desire to "preach the Gospel in the regions beyond you..." (2 Cor. 10:16 KJV).

---

1. Jer. 45:5; John 5:44, 12:43.

Developing and Maintaining Apostolic Ambition

I am often asked by Christians, "How do you keep the fire burning? How can you keep a real stoke going for the Lord and not burn out?" The key is in our understanding of God's calling on our lives.

Before New Testament times, an apostle was a commander of a fleet or a military expedition who was sent on an overseas mission. In Greek the word simply means "sent one." Paul never forgot that he had been personally commissioned by Jesus to take the good news to all nations. Well into his sixties, he was still pursuing that goal with the same fiery zeal he had when he first launched out from Damascus. In his letters to the Corinthians, we get some insight into three keys that made Paul tick and gave him the fire that burned brightly until he passed into glory.

Apostolic Priorities

Like us, Paul had hundreds of choices about good things he could do and places he could go in his ministry. He had to learn to listen to God's voice but also to watch for God's wisdom in setting priorities. He knew the decisions he made would affect his co-workers and the destiny of others as well. Here are some examples of Paul's apostolic guidelines:

1. The Gospel takes priority over human wisdom.

*"…the Greeks seek after wisdom: But we preach
Christ crucified, unto the Jews a stumblingblock,
and unto the Greeks foolishness"* (1 Cor. 1:22-23 KJV).

Paul was tempted to water down the Gospel message to satisfy the philosophical Greek mind, but he knew it would take away from its saving power. Obviously, Paul knew how to reason with intellectuals. His sermon to the Greek philosophers on Mars Hill proves this (Acts 17:22-31). He also "reasoned" with the Jews in the synagogue that Jesus was the Messiah. Whenever possible he tried to become "all things to all men" to win them to Christ. But whatever interest door he used to open the hearts of his hearers, the bottom line was always "Jesus Christ and Him crucified" (1 Cor. 2:2) as the power of God for salvation.

Spurgeon once told his students "I don't argue with people. I just lay down my straight rod next to their crooked stick and let them choose." God's ways are not always our ways (Isa. 55:8) and His wisdom is often antithetical to ours. For example, how about marching around Jericho or dipping in the Jordan seven times (Josh. 6; 2 Kings 5)? Or take the case of Gladys Aylward. She was deemed by mission boards to be too old, too small and too uneducated for the grueling life of a missionary. Her success in China proved that even the "foolishness of God is wiser than men" (1 Cor. 1:25).

2. The Gospel takes priority over human wants.

"...the Jews require a sign, and the Greeks seek after wisdom" (1 Cor. 1:22 KJV).

Paul's second apostolic priority was to resist the temptation to pander to everyone's "felt needs." Of course, we should recognize needs and meet them whenever possible, but often we let the secondary need replace the primary one. The Jews wanted signs but they had proven by their history that they could see signs galore and still not believe. The Greeks wanted wisdom but if Paul would have stooped to giving them a human-based philosophical Gospel he would have had to keep scratching their intellect to keep them "saved."

Some missionaries have allowed the wants of the people to replace the message of the Gospel, which is their primary need. More than one missionary society has, in the face of overwhelming need, allowed ministries of mercy, relief and development to become a substitute for the preaching of the Cross rather than a supplement to it. This misplaced priority, along with a liberal view of the Scriptures on heaven and hell, deals a lethal blow to the fulfillment of the Great Commission.

Don Stephens, director of Mercy Ships, has given the analogy of the "two-handed Gospel." The one hand is a hand of human compassion and love, ministering in mercy to needs wherever they are found. In the other hand is the Gospel of salvation, the message of God's love for sinners and an offer of forgiveness through the blood of the Cross. E. Stanley Jones, the great missionary to India, once said, "An individual gospel without a social gospel is a soul without a body. A social gospel is a body without a soul. The one is a ghost. The other is a corpse."

3. The Gospel takes priority over human workers.

> *"For while one saith, I am of Paul; and another, I am of Apollos; are ye not carnal?"* (1 Cor. 3:4 KJV).

The Corinthians, much like the church today, had a tendency to exalt human personalities over the priorities of the Gospel message. With all due respect to those mentors and Christian leaders who guide us along the Way, we must never forget who it is we're serving. More than one sincere disciple has lost his stoke because he put his faith and identity in a man or a movement and not in God Himself.

The Bereans were called "noble" because they searched the Scriptures daily to make sure the things the great Apostle Paul was teaching them were right. We must, of course, give honor where it is due (Rom. 13:7), but no matter who, or what the source, we must "test everything. Hold on to the good." (1 Thess. 5:21 NIV).

Paul warned the Ephesian elders that there would be those who would draw away disciples "after themselves" (Acts 20:30). We who are being discipled, and those of us who are mentors, must be sure we do not allow our "connection" to go beyond God's limits. Unhealthy dependence on another human being can only yield bad fruit. We don't need gurus. We need God.

4. The Gospel takes priority over human works.

> *"Every man's work shall be made manifest: for the day shall declare it, because it shall be revealed by fire; and the fire shall try every man's work of what sort it is"* (1 Cor. 3:13 KJV).

Paul understood that his Gospel *work* must flow out of his Gospel *walk*. His race must be run out of his relationship with the Lord. His fourth apostolic priority was on the quality of his work. The imagery of fire again paints a graphic picture of the temporal nature of combustible wood, hay and stubble as opposed to "gold, silver and precious stones" which would abide the fire of God's judgment (1 Cor. 3:12-15). Our work will be tested. When it is, motivation, not machismo, will determine whether our works are apostolic and able to survive the refiner's fire.

Using the picture of a building, Paul said that as an architect we must take heed *how* we build (1 Cor. 3:10). For our work to be apostolic it must be *Christ-centered*. He must be the foundation (1 Cor. 3:11), not our wisdom, wants, workers or denominational whims.

Another mark of apostolic work is that it's *focused*. The ultimate objective of all Gospel work should be the discipling of all the nations and thus filling the earth "with the knowledge of the glory of the Lord, as the waters cover the sea" (Hab. 2:14 NIV). The final mark of apostolic ministry is that its work is *lasting*. That is, it can abide the test of God's dealings, Satan's attacks and man's criticism. This is why the foundation and materials are so crucial.

Much Christian work seems to be built on the assumption that there will be no tomorrow. What a sad state the world would be in today if all believers embraced that assumption. We must build with the next generation in mind. He's given us a job to do, and until He returns we need to keep doing it. Our priorities must give way to God's priorities. And our human wisdom, wants, workers and works must take a back seat to God's ways and purposes.

This brings us to the subject of discipline—the second strand of the "three-fold cord" (Eccl. 4:12) that will fuel the fire of apostolic ambition.

Apostolic Discipline

"...I buffet my body and make it my slave, lest possibly, after I have preached to others, I myself should be disqualified" (1 Cor. 9:27 NAS).

Paul, knowing the imagery of Olympic-style games would be familiar to his Greek readers, spoke of the Christian life as an athletic contest—a race or a boxing match (1 Cor. 9:24-27). His point was that in the same way an athlete trains for his athletic event so we should discipline ourselves in the spiritual life for our "race" or "fight."[2]

We must put great diligence into developing habit patterns that will help us stay "under the glory spout where the glory comes out." Personal spiritual discipline is just that—discipline—and as such, it's sometimes difficult to develop and maintain. This is simply because our flesh, the world and the devil are all dead set against a disciplined Christian. Doing battle with a dedicated Christian soldier, who is disciplined and fully armed with God's weapons, is one of the devil's worst nightmares. The rewards and victories of a disciplined life are great, and as Paul put it, "...an uncorruptible crown..." awaits you (1 Cor. 9:25).

Much of what I have observed among "stale" or lukewarm Christians who have lost their ambition is simply a lack of personal discipline. Sure, we all go through dry periods, but they should make us thirst for God all the more. John 10:10 characterizes the normal Christian life as "abundant"—one that overflows and blesses others. So if your dry times are turning into dry seasons and dry years, you need to ask yourself some tough questions.

How hungry and thirsty are you for God and His righteousness? Do you value God's "pearl of great price" so much that you'll sacrifice all else to get it? David said "...my soul thirsteth for thee, my flesh longeth for thee in a dry and thirsty land, where no water is...because thy lovingkindness is better than life, my lips shall praise thee" (Psalm 63:1,3 KJV).

The application is obvious. If we truly *believe* His lovingkindness is better than life, we also will be thirsting after Him day and night. That desire for God leads us into discipline. That sounds easy, but make no mistake, discipline is hard work. It is the practice of making your body and mind do something that they don't

---

2. This theme is developed more fully in *Before You Hit The Wall*, Danny Lehmann (YWAM Publishing).

necessarily want to do. We are lazy by nature, especially when it comes to spiritual things. We'd much rather have God pursue us, than we pursue Him. But we must pursue Him. The amazing thing is that when we habitually channel our mind and body into the pursuit of God, these spiritual disciplines soon become a delight. The parallel with physical exercise again illustrates this point.

At present I run a marathon (26.2 miles) each December. I start semi-serious training around August 15th. I do speed work, distance work, hill training and to a limited degree, watch my diet (I'm still working on that one!). By the time of the race, I'm usually in good enough shape to rank in the top 2 percent of the finishers. My pattern has been to take a week or two off after the race to recuperate, then plunge into the Christmas holidays and all the culinary temptations that go with them.

When I start running again around the first week of January, it feels as if I've never run before. I feel sluggish, "fat" and out of shape. It's hard to get moving and motivated, and again it takes *discipline*. I can honestly say that running five miles on that first week of January is actually harder than running the marathon three weeks before. The difference is my conditioning. It still amazes me how fast you can lose it.

I've found the same is true of my spiritual "conditioning." When I go through a "slump" in my spiritual disciplines (the Word, prayer, fasting, etc.), I find it is that much harder to get back into sync once again. Hence the need for *consistent* spiritual discipline.

Paul was able to exhort his readers to pray without ceasing... give thanks in everything...give attention to Scripture reading...and to train like an athlete, take up weapons and armor like a soldier, and work hard like a farmer because he was consistently practicing these disciplines in his own life.[3]

Another important reason for apostolic discipline is that periodically we get hit by spiritual "earthquakes" that can reduce our Christian life and ministry to rubble if we're not prepared. In recent earthquakes in California, the difference between buildings that

---

3.   1 Thess. 5:17,18; 1 Tim. 4:13; 2 Tim. 2:3-6.

collapsed and those that withstood the shaking, was how well the infrastructure was reinforced. Our spiritual disciplines buttress us against trials and testings in the same way. Prayer, Bible study and worship put steel into our character.

You can start building yourself up spiritually by setting attainable, measurable goals. For instance, increase the time in your morning devotions. Keep in mind that God is not a cosmic score-keeper who's counting the minutes and milliseconds you spend in prayer. You may want to increase your average time by a few minutes. Experiment with your devotional life by waiting in His presence for five uninterrupted minutes, not saying a word, just waiting. Purchase a prayer diary or journal and learn to chart your spiritual progress and record your prayers. Try to sing "psalms and hymns and spiritual songs, singing with grace in your hearts to the Lord" (Col. 3:16 NKJV).

In the beginning, you probably won't feel like doing this. Remember, it's discipline. Tell the Lord you love Him, and budget time to spend with Him nurturing that love. Your love relationship with the Lord is similar in a sense to any friendship or marriage. It needs to be maintained.

Set other goals for Bible reading, Scripture memorization and Bible study. Discipline yourself to take notes in church and home group meetings to assimilate the teaching into your spirit. Read Christian books and biographies that will stoke your soul with love for God and build up your faith.

Take baby steps in the sometimes neglected disciplines of fasting, solitude, contemplation, meditation and Sabbath rest. If you are so bold, take inventory on the bodily disciplines of physical exercise and diet.

Paul's Spirit-inspired exhortation to Timothy to "discipline yourself for the purpose of godliness" (1 Tim. 4:7 NAS), and his Spirit-dominated example should provide extra stoke for us to get started on our own pursuit of God. This joyful daily adventure is what Richard Foster calls the *Celebration of Discipline* and Elisabeth Elliot dubs, *Discipline—The Glad Surrender.*[4]

---

4. Richard Foster, *Celebration of Discipline* (Harper and Row, 1978); Elisabeth Elliot, *Discipline—The Glad Surrender* (Fleming H. Revell, 1982).

Apostolic Strategy

The third strand of our three-fold cord is strategy. Some Christians balk at the word strategy because they think it implies a humanistic attempt to accomplish God's will. By strategy I simply mean appropriate use of the means God has given us to execute the commands He gives us. In His parables, Jesus spoke about strategy. The main point of the parable of the virgins is simple: The five wise virgins used good strategy, the five foolish ones used bad strategy. The parable of the talents and pounds is similar (Matt. 25, Luke 19).

Paul also had a strategy. It was based on the Holy Spirit's leading, biblical principles and Spirit-inspired common sense. For example, he chose to plant churches in strategically located trade cities of the Roman Empire. From there, the Gospel quickly spread. In Paul's second letter to the Corinthians, you get the feeling he is looking to the horizon when he writes of his desire "to preach the Gospel in the regions beyond you..." (2 Cor. 10:16 KJV). To reach the ends of the earth was his objective. His strategy was how he was planning to do it.

Clearly, the church needs strategies if we are ever to complete the Great Commission. It gives me great joy to see missions organizations like Target 2000, Caleb Project, and the U.S. Center for World Missions targeting unreached people groups. God is giving specific strategies for how to reach into those cultures with the Gospel.

God also gives strategies for our personal evangelism. My friend John Bills gave me an example I'll never forget. John felt God was leading him to reach out to terminally ill AIDS patients, and one was a young man named Skip. Upon discerning John was a Christian, Skip made it clear he had no interest in God. He said if John was to be his friend, he was *not* to witness to him.

This encounter left John perplexed so he sought God for a strategy. God's word to him was simply "love him." For the next several months, John did just that. He took him meals, transported him to doctors' appointments, and as the dreaded disease took more of its toll on Skip, helped him with various bathroom necessities. Tough love indeed.

One morning while in prayer, John had a strong impression to make chicken soup for Skip. As he approached the pantry to pull down a can of Campbell soup, God spoke to his heart, "No, *homemade* chicken soup." So with a little help from a Betty Crocker cookbook, John obeyed God, and took a thermos of homemade soup to Skip.

A few days later, Skip asked John what prompted him to make the soup. He added that on that particular morning he had awakened with an intense craving for homemade chicken soup like his mother used to make for him. John drew a breath and said, "You made it clear you don't want the Gospel pushed on you, and I've honored that request. The fact is though, I was praying for you that morning, and I felt like God told me to make you homemade chicken soup." Skip's eyes filled with tears.

Despite this opening, Skip still was reluctant to surrender to Jesus. John was feeling a new sense of urgency because Skip's condition was rapidly deteriorating. He knew he was in a battle for Skip's soul, and he fasted and cried out to God on his behalf. That Sunday morning, John received a call from the AIDS ward. "Please come immediately. Skip has taken a turn for the worse. He wants to see you."

John arrived to find Skip's bed surrounded by friends and medical people paying their last respects. John shuffled over to a corner and prayed one last desperate prayer, "God, please get rid of these people. They'll throw me out if I start witnessing to Skip." One by one, the people started leaving the room for one reason or another. When all were gone, John sat on Skip's death bed. Then with clasped hands he renounced his lifestyle, confessed his sins and surrendered to Jesus. The battle had been won. God's strategy of loving, sacrificial service and fervent prayer had defeated the enemy.

At different levels and in various areas, we, like Paul on Mars Hill or John in an AIDS ward, are engaged in spiritual warfare. And like them, we need to remember what we are fighting for, who we are fighting and where and when we need to dig in for battle. A Christian soldier with strong apostolic priorities, disciplines and strategies will be ready to raise God's standard when the enemy comes in like a flood (Isa. 59:19).

"Friendly" Fire

In using the analogy of soldiers in battle, I would be less than honest if I left the impression that we who are in Christ march on unscathed in every battle. We are assured of ultimate victory, but as in all battles, our combat with Satan will leave some casualties. A good soldier in God's army knows that and is ready to give his all. As Paul declared, "For me to live is Christ and to die is gain."

Unfortunately, not all casualties are caused by the enemy. One tragic reality of war is the occurrence of "friendly" fire. That is, when by mistake your own troops or planes open fire on you or you mistakenly fire on them. In the chaos, smoke, and fire of battle, we sometimes don't recognize who the enemy is. This happens most often when units attacking the same goal from different directions try to win the most victories or seize the most territory.

Paul understood the perils of friendly fire in the spiritual realm as well. He knew the tendency of the human heart towards competition and tried to keep himself and his troops from engaging in it:

"We dare not make ourselves of the number, or compare ourselves with some that commend themselves: but they measuring themselves by themselves, and comparing themselves among themselves, are not wise" (2 Cor. 10:12 KJV).

In Kingdom work we must not allow ourselves to get into a "performance" mode. For when we do we will always compare ourselves with others and ultimately compete against those who are in our own camp rather than our true adversary. If we compare ourselves with those whom we deem to be more spiritual, we'll feel condemned. If we compare ourselves with those whom we deem less spiritual, we'll be lifted up with pride. It's a no-win situation.

Tozer said, "We languish for men who feel themselves expendable in the warfare of the soul, who cannot be threatened with threats of death because they have already died to the allurements of this world. Such men will be free from the compulsions that control weaker men. This kind of freedom is necessary if we are to have prophets in our pulpits again, instead of mascots.

"These free men will serve God and mankind from motives too high to be understood by the rank and file or religious retainers, who today shuttle in and out of the sanctuary. They will make no decision out of fear, take no course out of a desire to please men, accept no service for financial considerations, nor will they allow themselves to be influenced by the love of publicity or the desire for reputation. He has nothing to protect, no ambition to pursue and no enemy to fear. For that reason, he is completely careless of his standing among men. If they follow him—well and good. If not, he loses nothing he holds dear, but whether he is accepted or rejected he will go on loving his people with sincere devotion and only death can silence his tender intercession for them."[5]

We must do battle against a competitive spirit by moving in the opposite direction. Quit trying to get all the credit you feel is due you for services rendered to the Kingdom. Learn to give glory away to others, even when they don't deserve it. Keep in mind we're all on the same team and in the same army.

Don't compete with your brothers and sisters. When others try to push you into competition, resist the devil by promoting the interests of the supposed "competition." And above all, as Gospel singer Chuck Girard has written, "Don't shoot the wounded, someday you might be one!"

One way to keep friendly fire at a minimum is to stay within your "sphere" of ministry. Keep in mind your ministry gifts, and don't get drawn into activities that are outside the ministry areas God has appointed for you. In other words, let's stay off other people's "turf." In doing so, we will not only keep from overextending ourselves, but greatly reduce the potential for conflict with other believers.

William Branham was one of the most successful healing evangelists in history. He stepped out of the sphere God had apportioned for him and began teaching theology. He had no theological education nor did he have a theological mind. He ended up being a proponent of the "Jesus only" doctrine which denies the Holy Trinity. He led thousands down this misguided theological path. In

---

5. A. W. Tozer, *Of God and Men* (Harrisburg, PA: Christian Publications).

all likelihood, this would never have happened if he had stayed within his sphere as an evangelist.

In the refreshingly transparent book, *The Man Who Could Do No Wrong*,[6] Charles Blair chronicles the subtle steps he took outside of his sphere as a pastor. His risky business dealings put his church several million dollars in debt. His motive was right—to build a home to help the elderly, but he was outside his sphere. He was convicted of several counts of fraud and given a 61-year prison term. The judge, by God's mercy, suspended the sentence so the Pastor could get back in his sphere (at the helm of his church) and help pay off the debt.

Paul understood that staying in his sphere was an effective strategy for reaching the "regions beyond." In another text on apostolic ambition, he told the Romans that he "aspired to preach the gospel, not where Christ was already named, that I might build upon another man's foundation; [i.e. to stay out of their sphere] but as it is written, 'They who had no news of him shall see and they that have not heard shall understand'" (Rom. 15:20-21 NAS).

So how is your ambition? Is it healthy, alive, fervent and focused on God's objective to making disciples of all nations? Whether you are crossing the sea or crossing the street to serve God, are you focused in prayer toward the frontiers? Or is your ambition in critical condition? If so, take it to Dr. Jesus. Lay down on the table and let him operate. By God's grace He'll answer your heart's cry and set you ablaze for Him.

---

6. Charles Blair, *The Man Who Could Do No Wrong*, (Lincoln, VA: Chosen Books, 1981).

Stoker quote

*"If you would make the greatest success
of your life, try to discover what God is
doing in your time and fling yourself into
the accomplishment of His purpose."*
Selected

Chapter Eleven

Generation X
and the 21st Century

*"For when David had served God's purpose
in his own generation, he fell asleep..."*
Acts 13:36 (NIV)

Martin Luther, who shook his generation with the truth of justification by faith, once said, "If you preach the Gospel and do not relate it to the issues of your time, you're not preaching the Gospel at all."

Luther's warning has tremendous application for us today as we move into the 21st century. The truth of the Gospel never changes, but how that truth is packaged and presented to each generation may vary. Street preaching and witnessing, friendship evangelism, mass crusades, rock concerts, Christian magic and comedy, "Power Team" exhibitions, mercy ministries and a host of other evangelistic methods have been blessed by God in reaching and winning the lost.

When Acts says David "served the purpose of God in his own generation and fell asleep," it seems clear to me that God has a purpose for each generation. Apparently, each new generation of

Christians is responsible for finding ways to reach the sinners of their generation and the one that follows. We must be like the "men of Issachar, who understood the times and knew what Israel should do" (1 Chron. 12:32 NIV).

What about this generation? What are some keys that might help us to understand what makes them tick? How can we best prepare ourselves to be instruments in the hands of a God who desperately wants to reach them? Perhaps these questions can be answered best by taking a look at the times and characteristics of the preceding generations.

Many sociologists call the generation born in the first 20 years of this century the "G.I. Generation," reflecting the dominating effect of World War I on all born during that era. Their world was shaken by events beyond their understanding or control. Then came the "Silent Generation," those born amid the Great Depression and continuing through World War II. Daily survival was their agenda in a world of bread lines and hand-to-mouth living.

The post-war generation—some 80 million of us—are affectionately called the "Baby Boomers." World War II soldiers came home and sired by far the largest single crop of kids in the nation's history. Children born during the 1946-1964 era entered a world of prosperity and possibilities. But new influences of television, rock music, drugs and sexual promiscuity, along with social upheaval from a new war and racial and gender rights issues, caused a strong sense of alienation.

The huge number of Baby Boomers has in itself created problems for the twenty-something generation that's been dubbed "Generation X." That term was coined by Douglas Coupland in a book called *Generation X*. It is a novel that reflects the frustrations and insecurities that plague the successors of the Baby Boomers. For instance, Coupland notes rather cynically that the "Baby Busters" must settle for low-paying, dead-end "McJobs" because the Boomers have saturated the job market. In sweeping narrative style, Coupland examines and lampoons the lifestyle and values of the generation as it struggles to find its own identity. Although it is fiction, Coupland's book is certainly based on reality.

Recent studies by *Time*, *Newsweek* and other magazines confirm that certain characteristics identified in Coupland's book distinguish Generation X from its ancestors. They include these:

1. Loss of Family Structure

Census figures show that under 10 percent of American homes represent the "typical" family of the post-war era. The old pattern of dad out earning the family income while mom stayed at home tending the 2.4 kids is a thing of the past. Economic pressures that have forced moms to work have dramatically increased the number of "latchkey kids" (those left unattended after school because mom and dad are at work). Domestic violence, divorce and parental abuse have made the concept of "one big, happy family" a rarity. This is not to mention the political and spiritual forces that are seeking to redefine what a family actually is.

2. Afraid of Relationships

In a 1994 *Time*/CNN poll, 58 percent of the Gen-Xers interviewed said they did not want to have a marriage like their parents. Recent census figures show that 75 percent of all 19-24 year old males still live at home—the largest percentage since the Great Depression. Since nearly 50 percent of them come from broken homes, this could account for their understandable paranoia about "permanent" relationships.

3. Unfocused

This generation is less career orientated than their Yuppie (young urban professional) forefathers. The *Time*/CNN survey shows that personal fulfillment, rather than financial prosperity is their goal. This is partly because the economic feeding frenzy of the 1980s glutted the job-market with Boomers who aren't exactly anxious to share their blessings with the next generation. Gen-Xers also may be less motivated because they've observed that their parents' striving after money didn't make them happy anyway.

They also seem to be a generation without a cause. Their parents protested the Vietnam War, fought for civil and women's rights and actually pulled off a cultural revolution.

But today's social and political issues just aren't grabbing the interest of the Xers. They are characterized by a lack of commitment and wanderlust. A full 60 percent interviewed in the *Time*/CNN survey said they want to travel extensively while they're young, mostly to exotic places like Kathmandu and Bangkok.

4. Lack of Social Glue

Much like the "cause" issue, this generation is struggling for an identity. They can't seem to come to a consensus on music or styles. Punk, metal, rap, reggae, Seattle grunge, and revived 1960s rock n' roll all compete for their loyalty. Their clothing styles reflect at once the Levi's and T-shirt look of their parents, the "skater" baggy look, khakis and Republican three-piece suits. Even tie-dyes and bell bottoms are making a comeback. It's the same with hair styles. A tour of any high school will reveal long hair, the shaved "East L.A. homeboy" look, the greased back ponytail look, side fenders and even a few mohawks left over from the early '80s, Individualism, not conformity, is the operative word.

5. No Heroes

In the survey taken by *Time*/CNN, no more than 10 percent of this generation can agree on a hero. They don't relate to political and social figures like the Boomers did with the Kennedys and Martin Luther King. The now-tarnished image of those men seems to have dealt a blow to the concept that anyone could truly champion the cause of a generation.

They do admire some movie, music and sports idols. Michael Jackson and Madonna once attempted generational hero status, only to be shot down in flames by their off-stage lifestyles. Other scandals in the political, religious and sports worlds have nailed shut the coffin on heroism for the Gen-Xers.

The main characteristic of Generation X may be that it is so hard to figure out. Adjectives like hopeless, aimless, wandering, and even apathetic and lazy have been used to describe this crop of young people coming up in the ranks.

Evangelist Mario Murillo has identified four events in U.S. history that he believes have helped cause the aimlessness of Generation Xers. Ironically, most sociologists identify these events with the Baby Boomers. The line of demarcation between the "Boomer" and "Buster" generations is usually set at 1962-1964. Now consider these significant events that happened in that short window of time:

The Vietnam war—The war bitterly divided the country and destroyed a nation's trust in its authorities.

The Kennedy assassination—The November 1963 assassination of a popular U.S. President shook the nation to its core. For many it was the loss of a role model who symbolized hope for the future. Others saw an evil conspiracy in the suspicious events surrounding the assassination. The many doubts galvanized into a collective consciousness about Kennedy that we refuse to lay to rest.

The Beatles invasion—You may scoff at the U.S. debut of the British pop stars in February 1964 as a major sociological event, but their music and lifestyle significantly influenced the nation. I'm not accusing the Beatles of any evil intent, but they represented a change in our culture characterized by drugs, eastern mysticism and sexual promiscuity.

School prayer decision—Although usually overlooked by the sociologists, the Supreme Court ruling in 1963 that prayer be taken out of public schools is a watershed event in our history. The effect of keeping millions of school children from praying for God's blessing on our nation cannot be underestimated. Only eternity will reveal its devastating toll on the moral and spiritual fabric of our country.

These four explosions within two years of each other scored a direct hit on the values of the Boomer generation, and they weakened the foundations of the generation to come. The wandering, unfocused generation that emerged is indeed lost, but they are not hopelessly lost.

I have tremendous hope for this generation for the very reason that many people have given up on them. Because our God delights to do those things we consider impossible! He is the God who said to Ezekiel, "Can these [dry] bones live?" And then He breathed His Spirit on them and raised them up as a mighty army (Ezk. 37:1-14).

God has a plan for Generation X. He wants to breathe His Spirit on them and use them as an unstoppable force that will crush the enemy and complete the Great Commission.

Consider the following scenario:

The generation that leads us into the 21st century, which grew up without the benefit of prayer in school, suddenly becomes a militant force of righteousness because they rediscover the secret of prevailing prayer for revival. Fresh fire from Heaven descends as it did on the day of Pentecost. Then the Scripture is fulfilled that says, "your young men [Generation X males] shall see visions, and your old men [Baby Boomers] shall dream dreams: and on my servants and on my handmaidens [Generation X females] I will pour out in those days of my Spirit, and they shall prophesy" (Acts 2:17-18 KJV).

The generation that lost its faith in authority figures, then humbly submits to Him Who has all authority on Heaven and on Earth. Their aimlessness and wanderlust is transformed into a fervent desire to take the Gospel to the ends of the Earth. The generation without a cause discovers the greatest cause of all—taking the Gospel of the Kingdom to every nation on the planet.

The generation that lacks family structure and is afraid of relationships rediscovers God's design for the family. Husbands, fathers, wives, mothers and children take their proper place in God's order for the home. Teenagers start believing that true love can wait, and chastity and virginity again become virtues in a society reaping the consequence of moral insanity. The fire of God's holiness and love melt the hardness and pride that breaks relationships. Humility, brokenness and transparency mold us into a single-minded worldwide family with a deep desire to impact whole nations for God.

The generation that had to grow up settling for heroes like Kurt Cobain and Michael Jackson becomes enamored with Him Who is the Ultimate Hero—the Lord Jesus Christ. He will take His rightful place on the throne of the heart of all the Gen-Xers who call upon His name. They will love Him supremely and worship Him absolutely. They will allow Him, by the "washing of the water of the Word" of God, to cleanse them from sin, fuel their faith and thus prepare a bride for Himself that is "without spot or wrinkle or any such thing" (Eph. 5:27 RSV).

Jesus will then wipe every tear from their eyes, and wipe the "X" off their collective memory forever. They will rejoice for all eternity. For God all along intended to confound those who had written them off by giving this generation the unspeakable privilege of seeing the final outpouring of God's glory—an outpouring that will amaze even the angels.

Now, that's something to get stoked about! Those of us in the Boomer generation need to start seeing Generation X through eyes of faith and praying this scenario into existence.

Timothy, The Last Days and Generation X

I have often wondered what I would preach and how I would conduct myself if I knew I was shortly going to die. Two New Testament books that give insight into "going-away" teaching are Paul's last two epistles. In these letters to Timothy, his "beloved son in the faith," the aged apostle indicates that he knew his time on earth was short (2 Tim. 4:6). The issues Paul emphasizes in these "last days" letters give us some clues about how we can pass our faith to the next generation.[1]

Timothy seems to be an excellent prototype of a first century Generation Xer. He was young, insecure, timid and apparently even physically weak (1 Tim. 5:23). He was the product of a mixed marriage and apparently spent at least some of his youth being raised

---

1. I am a firm believer, as indicated earlier, that Jesus can return at any time. I am planning, however, to do my best to "occupy until He comes" (Lk. 19:13). Luther once said when asked what he would do if he knew Christ was returning tomorrow, "I'd plant a tree!"

by a single mom, a strong Christian, with some influence from his grandmother (2 Tim. 1:5).[2]

He needed to be challenged to fight for his faith and for the truth of the Gospel, and to choose to be strong in the Lord. Paul warned Timothy that in the last days there would be a falling away from the faith, or apostasy (1 Tim. 4:1-3). Apparently alongside God's plan to pour out His Spirit on all mankind, Satan has a parallel plan, which would be implemented by "deceiving spirits and things taught by demons" (1 Tim. 4:1 NIV).

The obvious weapon against the false teaching is the truth of the Gospel. Paul reminded Timothy of his upbringing in the Scriptures (2 Tim. 3:15-16). In 1 Timothy, he also warned him there would be distractions along the way to keep him from his destiny as a "good minister of Jesus Christ." These included "endless genealogies" and "old wives tales." He lets him know that the narrow way isn't an easy way.

In our day there are similar temptations and distractions. Both blatant temptations to sin and the "innocent amusements" that steal our time need to be avoided like the plague.

The stage is being set for the final culmination of events leading up to the fulfillment of all the prophecies regarding the end times. Jesus warned of false Christs, false prophets and other signs of the times, including wars, earthquakes, an intense outpouring of hatred, betrayal and bloodshed. Compromising Christians will be plentiful (Matt. 24:3-14).

The battle lines are being drawn. Even in America, Christians and what they stand for are being viewed with increasing contempt. What once were grey areas are being obliterated by a more vivid black and white. The Lord of the harvest calls out today as He did in the days of Moses, "Who is on the Lord's side?" (Ex. 32:26 KJV). How will you respond?

---

2. In Acts 16, Luke writes that Timothy's father "was a Greek." The imperfect tense of the verb "was" has led some scholars to believe his father had been dead for some time when Paul first encountered him. (J. R. W. Stott, *The Spirit, The Church and the World* [I. V. P., 1990] 254.)

The Timothy Principle

As Paul neared his death, one of his last exhortations to Timothy was for him to train other faithful men. Timothy was told to look for disciples under his charge in whom he saw potential for leadership. The idea was for Timothy to prioritize his time and energy and concentrate on mentoring those who displayed character qualities such as faithfulness, loyalty and integrity. He was to train them to know God and to make Him known to others. Those mentored by Timothy were then to train others to do the same.

This "Timothy Principle" is the same strategy that Jesus gave His disciples on the Mount of Olives shortly before His ascension; "Go therefore and make disciples of all nations…teaching them to observe all that I commanded you…" (Matt. 28:19,20 NAS). God's genius is shown in the utter simplicity of the Great Commission. The experience of planting and nurturing the life of Jesus in a young person stokes me every time. We are called to make disciples who are equipped to make disciples of others.

There are numerous books on disciple-making that can give lots of the how-to's of mentoring this next generation. Some that I would recommend include *Mentoring for Mission* by Gunter Krallman, *The Master Plan of Evangelism* by Robert Coleman, and *The Lost Art of Disciple-Making* by Leroy Eims. I will not attempt to add to or improve upon the volumes that these and others have written about discipling. I will simply close by saying DO IT! I challenge both the grandparents and the Boomers to light a fire that will burn in the next generation.

Boomers Rise Up

In 1993, I attended the funeral of my dear friend Lonnie Frisbee, who was used by God to win thousands of young people to Christ during the Jesus Movement. The sadness of his early departure at age 43 was deepened in me as I exchanged greetings with other former Jesus People that day. Some were still blazing for God, but many had lost their stoke. I saw former disciples who once were on the cutting edge of revival now living in spiritual mediocrity. Others had abandoned their call and had backslid into immorality.

Usually they pointed fingers at others as the cause of their demise. That day at the Crystal Cathedral, a burden rested on me that helped confirm my decision to write this book.

Not only in America, but in many parts of the world there was a great outpouring of the Spirit on the youth in the early 1970s. Those young people are now in their 30's and 40's and are in a prime position to mentor leaders from the new generation. The church needs those leaders. Just look at the average age of the leaders in churches and parachurch organizations, and you'll see an abundance of Boomers and a dearth of twenty-somethings. One reason for this disparity is that Baby Boomers still idolize youth and refuse to grow up. We must get our feelings adjusted to the facts. Time's a wastin' and there is a whole new generation that needs to be reached.

We must prepare them and make way for them. Let's start prioritizing our time to give them the guidance and input they need to catch a vision for their world. *Time* magazine's assessment is that this generation needs more feedback, affirmation and encouragement than their forefathers. If that's what they need, let's give it to them. If they are not self-starters, let's help them get started. If they need a challenge, let's give it to them, but be careful not to bury them in the process.

To a large degree, the success we have in spreading the fire of God into the 21st century will depend on whether we start now to invest in our young people. Former Jesus People need to rise up and be counted. In my travels, I have met hundreds of weary, wary and wounded mid-lifers who have all but given up on having an impact for God. Most just don't know where they can plug in. The outlets are there, believe me. Humble yourself, Mr. and Mrs. Baby Boomer, be a servant and serve in the church ministry God leads you to. You'll find that the "…glory of this house will be greater than…the former" (Hag. 2:9 NAS).

Above all, pray for this generation. Pray for individuals you know; pray for youth groups and leaders; pray for an outpouring of God's holy fire on the whole generation. Pray without ceasing until God brings it to pass!

Blotting Out the "X"

The challenge for the leaders of the 21st century will be first of all to believe what God says about them, rather than what secular sociologists, psychologists and even Satan himself have to say. The label "Generation X" and their characteristic apathy, laziness, aimlessness, hopelessness, self-pity and self-centeredness are hauntingly similar to Paul's description of end-times people: "But mark this: There will be terrible times in the last days. People will be lovers of themselves, lovers of money, boastful, proud, abusive, disobedient to their parents, ungrateful, unholy, without love, unforgiving, slanderous, without self-control, brutal, not lovers of the good, treacherous, rash, conceited, lovers of pleasure rather than lovers of God—having a form of godliness but denying its power" (2 Tim. 3:1-5 NIV).

If you are a young person, you may think you are doomed to this kind of end, but that's not God's intent at all. He wants you and others of your "last-days" generation to be sure your world-view and self-view line up with Scripture. The fact is, you are not an "X" generation. You may be a product of it, but now, if you are born again "…old things are passed away; behold all things are become new…" (2 Cor. 5:17 KJV).

You are now a part of a new, redeemed community. God has called you *out* of darkness and out of the aimlessness that characterized a generation that has forgotten God. You are now called to go back into that generation—to bring them the fire of God's love and to snatch as many from the darkness as possible.

Just because you may have been raised on MTV doesn't mean your brains are made of marshmallows or that you can't learn the ways of God. He has put His Spirit within and empowered you to do things you never thought possible. You can "discipline yourself unto godliness" (1 Tim. 4:7). You can "be diligent to show yourself approved unto God…" (2 Tim. 2:15). You can present to God the raw combustible material that will allow Him to send fire down from heaven to ignite you. You can get stoked on Jesus. The question is, how badly do you want it?

Seek out a Christian you respect and ask him or her to mentor you. If you don't have a mentor readily available to disciple you, spend time alone with the Lord to get counsel directly from Him. Timothy did have his Paul, but there came a time when Paul left Timothy at Ephesus (1 Tim. 1:3). There, Timothy was "on his own" with the promise that as he obeyed the Great Commission, the Lord would be with him always. There is a time when our Elijah gets taken from us and we Elishas need to cross the Jordan alone (2 Ki. 2). God invites our cries for help and He will never leave us.

Real zeal and fire for God is part of your inheritance as a child of God. You may have been born into Generation X but you've been born again into a Kingdom that blots out any sins, hurts, or "X"s next to your name. You are valuable to God; first, because He created you in His image and secondly, because He redeemed you by His blood. He has a place for you in His Kingdom—not only for you, but for all those you will bring with you into His Kingdom. Yes, unless the Lord returns soon, you will need to disciple those born in the generation of the 1980s and 1990s. They have been dubbed "The 13th Generation" (and you thought the term Generation X was an insult!). This refers not only their position behind the Xers, but their "bad luck" to be born in such a crazy era. Who will see to it that they have an opportunity to see and experience God's cleansing power? Who will get them stoked?

A generation ago, a fast-living, hard-drinking rock star named Jim Morrison sang a song that became an anthem for a youth culture stoked on counterfeit fire. He cried out, "Come on baby, light my fire!" Tragically, he died of a drug overdose at age 27 and typified a generation going down in flames. Now we are looking into the young, fresh faces of a new generation that's also searching for answers. Will you help them find *the* answer?

King David, who served the purpose of God in his generation, wrote prophetically of a promise that God the Father made to God the Son. "The Lord said to my Lord, 'Sit at my right hand until I make your enemies a footstool for your feet.' The Lord will extend your mighty scepter from Zion; you will rule in the midst of your enemies. Your troops will be willing on your day of battle. Arrayed in holy majesty, from the womb of the dawn you will receive the dew of your youth" (Ps. 110:1-3 NIV).

As one of his soldiers, will you willingly volunteer on His day of battle? Will you help Him receive the "dew of His youth"? Will you be stoked on Jesus, committed to passionately loving Him and making Him known? If so, then I challenge you to boldly ask the Lord to fill you afresh with fervent love, real zeal and pure, unfiltered stoke.

COME ON, LORD, LIGHT MY FIRE!

Praying through the "window"

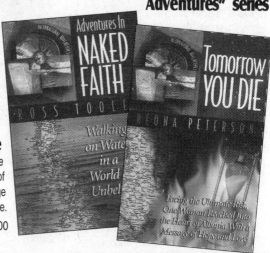